Properties

Properties

Douglas Edwards

polity

First published in 2014 by Polity Press

Polity Press
65 Bridge Street
Cambridge CB2 1UR, UK

Polity Press
350 Main Street
Malden, MA 02148, USA

ISBN-13: 978-0-7456-6174-2
ISBN-13: 978-0-7456-6175-9(pb)

A catalogue record for this book is available from the British Library.

Typeset in 10.5 on 12 pt Sabon
by Toppan Best-set Premedia Limited
Printed and bound in Great Britain by T.J. International Ltd, Padstow, Cornwall

The publisher has used its best endeavours to ensure that the URLs for external websites referred to in this book are correct and active at the time of going to press. However, the publisher has no responsibility for the websites and can make no guarantee that a site will remain live or that the content is or will remain appropriate.

Every effort has been made to trace all copyright holders, but if any have been inadvertently overlooked the publisher will be pleased to include any necessary credits in any subsequent reprint or edition.

For further information on Polity, visit our website: www.politybooks.com

To Mum and Dad

Contents

Preface

The world is populated with many different objects: tables, chairs, roses, fire engines, blades of grass and human beings, to name just a few, each occupying its own special region of space–time. When we distinguish between them, though, we often don't just make use of the idea that they exist in different locations; we also talk about the different features, attributes, or *properties* that they have. For instance, you and I have the property of being human, whereas tables and chairs do not. Roses and fire engines have the property of being red (or at least some do), whereas blades of grass do not. Conversely, the properties that objects have also help us to make sense of the ways in which distinct objects are *similar*: roses and fire engines are similar in an important way, as you and I are, because of the properties they – and we – share. However, positing the existence of properties immediately raises some interesting metaphysical questions. For example, how do we make sense of the idea that the redness of a fire engine is *the same* as the redness of a rose, when the fire engine and the rose exist in different places? Does this mean that one thing – the property *redness* – exists in different places at once, and, if so, how?

Understanding properties has been one of the main tasks of metaphysicians since the ancients, and a number of innovative proposals have been put forward. The aim of this book is to provide an accessible introduction to the main theories of properties: the view that properties are universals; the view that properties are constructed from tropes; and the view that properties are classes or sets of objects. We will chart these central positions in the debate and more, and we will note their strengths and weaknesses. We will address the main challenge to views that take properties seriously – that posed by Quine – which argues, contrary to what we said above, that we do not need properties to do any interesting explanatory work. We will address the question of what a theory of properties is intended to do, and we will take seriously the question of whether any single theory of properties is able to account for all the features that properties have been taken to have. We will also explore the connections between debates about properties and debates elsewhere in philosophy.

The first chapter introduces the topic under discussion and explores the main reasons for positing the existence of properties, including the 'one over many' argument. It then raises the question of what the constraints on a theory of properties are by considering the various jobs properties have been taken to do, before making some terminological distinctions. The second chapter discusses perhaps the most well-known view of properties, namely the view that properties are universals, and assesses both the transcendental view, attributed to Plato and developed by Bertrand Russell, and the immanent view, attributed to Aristotle and developed recently by David Armstrong. The third chapter introduces and assesses the view that properties are to be accounted for in terms of tropes. The fourth chapter assesses Quine's scepticism about properties and addresses his challenge to the theories under discussion in this book, which states that there are *no* properties at all. The fifth chapter explores various forms of nominalism about properties, particularly predicate nominalism, concept nominalism, class nominalism, mereological nominalism and resemblance nominalism. These views are all varieties of 'nominalism', as they deny – or at least claim to deny – the existence of universals or tropes. The sixth chapter explores pluralist approaches to properties, in particular David Lewis's influential distinction between 'abundant' and 'natural' properties. Finally, the seventh chapter examines some of the roles properties have in other debates in philosophy and discusses how the different accounts of properties explored in previous chapters might be affected.

As will become clear as we go through the book, we will rarely come across knock-down arguments against a view. Instead, the pattern that will become familiar is that each view has its own benefits and its own costs. Accordingly, the evaluation of competing views often takes the form of a cost/benefit analysis, and the choice of the view to adopt may not be particularly clear-cut. This is especially so in the case of the views under discussion in Chapters 2, 3 and 5, where we will see that different views privilege different reasons for positing the existence of properties. The views offered in Chapter 6 are designed to rectify this matter somewhat by attempting to show that incorporating different aspects of the previously discussed views into a new conception of properties can yield some progress. Whether they ultimately succeed, however, is a matter for debate.

I have approached this book as one does a series of philosophy lectures, in that the aim is to give a good understanding of the topic and to leave the audience primed and ready to investigate the subject, and the texts discussed, in greater depth. To this end I have included further reading lists at the end of each chapter, in addition to references throughout the main text. Many of the key texts in twentieth-century work on properties that are discussed are collected in D. H. Mellor and Alex Oliver's edited volume *Properties* (Oxford University Press, 1997). To make it easier for those who are using that book to find references in the text, for all the quotations from works reprinted in it I have included – apart from the page number of the original text – a reference to the corresponding page number in Mellor and Oliver. In some cases where the location of the original articles is hard to come by, I only have used the references to page numbers in the reprinted versions in the Mellor and Oliver volume, but included the full references in the bibliography.

I would like to thank Emma Hutchinson and Pascal Porcheron at Polity for their help and guidance during the whole process of writing this book. I am extremely grateful to Stephan Torre and two anonymous reviewers for Polity for providing very detailed comments on the manuscript, along with Manuela-Maria Tecusan for copy-editing the text. I am also grateful to three anonymous reviewers for Polity for feedback on the initial proposal. I would like to thank Maria Baghramian, Michael Lynch and Crispin Wright for their advice and encouragement, and members of the Aporo Metaphysics group in Dublin and the NIP Pluralism seminar in Aberdeen for a number of useful conversations. Earlier versions of some of the material here were presented, with great benefit to the book, at the University of Manchester, University College Dublin, the University of Aberdeen and the University of Sassari. I would also like to acknowledge funding from the Irish Research Council for the Humanities and Social Sciences and a Marie Curie Intra European Fellowship within the 7th European Community Framework programme. Finally, I would like to thank Alexandra Plakias, who read and commented on many versions of the manuscript and was an invaluable interlocutor during many helpful discussions, and my parents, who provided moral support throughout, as always.

1
Introducing Properties

1.1 Why Think that There Are Properties?

In this book we will be primarily concerned with theories which try to give an account of the *nature* of properties. Before we get that far though, we need first of all to consider why we might have to give such an account of properties at all. In other words, we need to pose the question of why we should think that there are properties. There are perhaps three main reasons for thinking that properties exist: (1) the one over many argument; (2) the reference argument; and (3) the quantification argument. The one over many argument is what we might call a *metaphysical* argument: it argues for the existence of properties on the basis of considerations of what the world must be like. As we will see, this is different from what the reference argument aims to do, which is to provide an argument for the existence of properties stemming from the structure of language – in other words to provide a *semantic* argument for the existence of properties. It is a more complex matter to characterise the quantification argument, as, depending on how one sees the ideas expressed, that one is something of a mixture between the first two – the metaphysical and the semantic argument.

We will revisit these three reasons as we go through the book, particularly as not all those who write on the subject think that they have equal weight (if any weight at all); but let us have a look at them here first.

1.1.1   The One over Many Argument

The one over many argument holds that we need to posit the existence of properties in order to respond adequately to the one over many *problem*. In our everyday experience we become acquainted with many particular objects, each occupying its own region of space–time. For instance, you – a particular object – currently hold a particular book, are probably sitting in a particular chair, and there are particular photons of light making it possible for you to read. In view of this, it is tempting to say that only particular things exist. However, it does not take much to show that this idea runs into some problems. We can take it that many particular things exist, but it also seems that many different particular things share the same nature. For instance, you and I are distinct objects, but we both seem to share something significant: we are both human beings. Indeed you might think that this is something that is *essential* to both of us: we would not be the objects we are unless we were human. This suggests that we are, both, the same *type* of thing. Putting the point more technically, you might say that we are, both, *tokens* of the same *type*: we are, both, particular tokens of the type *human being*.

We can also notice that this is the case even when objects are of a certain kind despite not being part of that kind essentially. For instance fire engines, roses and London buses are all distinct objects, but seem to share something in common, namely that they are all red. Notice, though, that they are not red essentially: fire engines, roses and London buses may have turned out not to be red, but the fact remains that they are all red, and thus they seem to be tokens of the type of red things.

We have said that individual objects such as you and I exist, so there should not be any harm in saying that the *tokens* in question exist. But should we also say that the *type* exists? If we say that it does, then we can make sense of the idea that we are both tokens *of* something, but at the cost that we no longer just admit the existence of particular objects: we must also admit the existence of *types*, which, it seems, do not exist in one particular region of space–time. If we deny the existence of types, however, then we maintain that only particular objects exist, but seemingly at the cost of being unable to say how it is that you and I are the same.

Returning to our talk of objects and properties, we can say that being of the same type entails the sharing of a property: objects that are tokens of a type have a property in common. Thus all the objects that are tokens of the type *human* share the property of being human; all the objects that are tokens of the type *red* share the property of being red. We can then translate the problem into talk of properties: do particular objects have properties? If so, then we can make sense of objects having characteristics in common, but at the cost of admitting non-object things into our ontology. If not, then we maintain the particularity of existence, but seemingly at the cost of being unable to hold that distinct objects have features in common.

The one over many *problem*[1] thus takes it that different objects are of the same type (whether essentially or not), and holds that this is a problem if we stick to a perhaps intuitive ontological view which just posits the existence of particular objects. The one over many *argument* for properties takes positing the existence of properties as a solution to this problem. The one over many argument thus holds that, in order to make proper sense of the things that exist, we must accept that properties as well as objects exist. In other words, it takes into account that we need to accommodate the idea that different individual objects are, and can be, of the same type (whether essentially or not), and that the best way to explain this is to posit the existence of properties as well as the existence of objects. Evidently the work does not stop here, as positing the existence of entities that seem to exist in a number of different places at the same time seems to throw up more questions than it answers; but these are issues we will discuss in the coming chapters.

We can also note that the one over many argument is a *metaphysical* argument, as it is drawn from a puzzle about *what exists*. This is the main problem we will focus on; but it is perhaps worth noting that there is a distinct *semantic* version of the argument that occasionally surfaces in the literature. The semantic version of the argument begins by asking a slightly different question: why is it that we apply the same predicate to many different objects? For instance, take the predicate 'is red'. This is one predicate, but it applies to a multitude of different things: fire engines, roses, Rudolph's nose, and so on. We might take *this* – the fact that we apply the same predicate to many different objects – to be in need of explanation.

Notice, though, that this is not the same problem as the one we have just discussed. That problem was a problem about *what exists*, and a solution to it will have to offer some account of what does and what does not exist. But this other problem is a problem about why we use items of language in a particular way, and a solution to it need not say anything about what exists. We *might*, of course, answer the question in such a way as to make claims about what exists – as we would if we were to say that the reason why we apply the predicate in each case is that each of the objects instantiates the same property; but we need not do so. We might, for example, offer a psychological explanation of why we use the same word for different objects, and this need not make any significant claims about what exists. For these reasons we will work with the *metaphysical* version of the one over many argument.

1.1.2   The Reference Argument

The reference argument, as noted above, is what we might call a *semantic* argument for the existence of properties, in that it uses considerations of language to argue that properties exist. The central idea is that we must posit the existence of properties to make sense of the meanings of certain kinds of linguistic entity; and there are two strands to this argument, stemming from two different kinds of linguistic entity. The first, and perhaps most prominent, idea is that we need properties to understand the meanings of *predicates*. The second is that we need properties to understand the meanings of a certain class of *singular terms*.

Singular terms (as the name suggests) are terms that have a unique referent. Classic examples are proper names (such as 'Jane Austen') and definite descriptions (such as 'the writer of *Pride and Prejudice*'). Each of these terms picks out a single and unique entity. We will call the referents of singular terms 'objects' to signify that they are distinct entities. Standard declarative sentences that philosophers tend to take interest in are formed of a singular term and a predicate, which we can express generally as '*a* is F'. Here '*a*' is the *subject term* of the sentence, typically a singular term, and 'is F' is the *predicate term* of the sentence. Some examples of sentences of this pattern are 'snow is white', 'the substance is alkaline', 'Jane Austen is human'. In cases of this sort, the subject term of the sentence picks out an object and the predicate term provides some description of that object. The sentence is true just in case the object picked out fits the description given by the predicate term. As we shall see, the referents of predicate terms are more contentious than the referents of subject terms, but, for now, we shall say that subject terms refer to *objects* and predicate terms refer to *properties*. That is, in the sentence 'Jane Austen is human', the subject term refers to Jane Austen and the predicate term refers to the *property* of being human. The sentence as a whole says that the object Jane Austen has the property of being human.

We have looked, then, at two basic components of language: predicates and singular terms. The reference argument takes as a basic premise that each linguistic entity of these two sorts refers to something. In most cases, for singular terms, this will be some existing object – which serves as the referent of that term. For predicates, it seems as though we cannot simply use objects; for, as we have seen, objects are singular entities, whereas predicates ascribe the same thing to many different objects. Properties, however, would seem to be good candidates to serve as referents of predicates: the predicate 'is red' is something that is predicated of many things, and we can equally well say that the property of being red is possessed by many different things. As a consequence, we get the natural semantic picture mentioned above, in which singular terms refer to objects, predicates refer to properties, and those properties are ascribed to objects.

One strand of the reference argument, then, is that we need to posit the existence of properties to serve as the referents for predicate terms in our language. However, we can note that we also find a certain kind of singular terms, which seem to refer to properties instead of objects. Consider the following series of sentences, given by David Lewis:

(1)   Red resembles orange more than it resembles blue.
(2)   Red is a colour.
(3)   Humility is a virtue.
(4)   Redness is a sign of ripeness. (Lewis 1983: 348/1997: 194)

Here we see terms like 'red' and 'humility' appearing in the singular term position of a sentence – and in a seemingly innocuous fashion, as all of these sentences seem to be unproblematically true. But, if we are taking objects to be entities that have a single spatiotemporal location, then it seems difficult to say that the singular terms in (1)–(4) refer to objects, as redness and humility seem to be things that are found in a number of different places at once. However, on the semantic picture we are operating with, they must refer to *something*, otherwise the sentences would not come out as true. As a result, we might wish to say that, for a certain class of singular terms – sometimes referred to as *abstract singular terms* – the proper referent is not an object, but a property. Thus the singular terms in (1)–(4) can be taken to refer to properties. This also shows – as should be clear – that properties can also have features predicated of them, and thus they can themselves have properties. This is, then, the second strand of the reference argument, which holds that we need to posit the existence of properties to serve as the referents of abstract singular terms.

1.1.3   The Quantification Argument

The reference argument argues for the existence of properties from a particular theory of meaning, which assigns entities to serve as the meanings of linguistic items. The quantification argument proceeds along similar lines, but without the need for a particular theory of meaning. Thus it can serve either as a complement to the reference argument or as a separate argument altogether.

The argument proceeds from some considerations of *ontological commitment*, which ask when we are committed to the existence of a particular entity, or kind of entities. A popular answer, and one we will explore in more detail in Chapter 4, is that one is committed to the existence of the entities that one *quantifies over* when making true statements. This is different from the reference argument, as there need not be any explicit reference to the entities in the given sentences. For example, consider the following sentences, also from David Lewis:

(5)   He has the same virtues as his father.
(6)   The dresses were of the same colour.
(7)   There are undiscovered fundamental physical pro-
        perties.
(8)   Acquired characteristics are never inherited.
(9)   Some zoological species are cross-fertile. (Lewis 1983: 350/1997: 196)

These sentences, if true, all have existential commitments. For example (5) entails that there exist *some* virtues that are shared between the individual and his father, and (6) entails that there exists *some* colour that both the dresses have. So the thought is, if (5)–(9) are to be considered true, then there must exist entities of the type mentioned. However, as we saw with the reference argument, it is, at least on the face of it, hard to see how objects could serve as the things that must exist here. Virtues, for example, don't seem to be the kind of things that would be considered objects; rather they seem like features that various objects can exhibit. The same goes, as we have seen, for colours, and also – plausibly – for acquired characteristics and zoological species. So, again, it looks as though properties would be better suited to be things that are required to exist if these sentences are to come out true. If this is so, then we have another argument for the existence of properties.

1.2   What Is a Theory of Properties?

We have looked, then, at some of the arguments which suggest that we need to take the existence of properties seriously. In the rest of the book we will explore the various theories that have been proposed to account for them (or indeed to explain them away). Before we do so, though, it is worth pausing to consider what a *theory* of properties is and what it might hope to achieve.

The theories of properties that we will be looking at are all trying to give some account of the *nature* of properties; they try to tell us what properties *are*. Sometimes this will be done in the form of attempting to show how properties are reducible to other kinds of entities (such as classes), other times it will be done differently. Broadly speaking, though, this project – of trying to explain the *nature* of properties – is the focus of the present book. This is not to say that the task of accounting for what properties *do* will be ignored: on the contrary, it is an important part of the project of accounting for what properties *are* that we consider what properties *do*.

1.3   A Methodological Strategy

If we want to give a theory of something, we need first to have some idea of what the thing is that we are trying to give a theory of – just as, if we want to find something, we need to have some idea of what it is we're looking for. For example, if a sheriff wants to find Mahoney, a dangerous criminal, she constructs a 'Wanted' poster that depicts the key features of Mahoney, which mark him out as Mahoney – such as, say, a scar across his cheek or a tattoo reading 'Mum' on his left biceps. These features serve as a guide to finding Mahoney: if we come across an individual that exhibits these features, we can be pretty sure that we've found him.

A popular approach to philosophical analysis suggests that we do the same with subjects philosophers are interested in. One test case for this can be found in the study of pain. Suppose that we want to know what pain is. We might start by listing all of the things that are distinctive of pain (pain is caused by tissue damage, pain causes people to say 'ouch!', pain is generally unpleasant, and so forth). Once we have a complete list of features such as these, we have a 'Wanted' poster for pain: we know what it is we are looking for. What we then need to do is look, for example, at the physical states of human beings and find which state is activated when a person exhibits the characteristic features of pain; and then we will have found pain. This kind of approach constitutes what is called a 'functionalist' approach to philosophical analysis (and it will be explored further in Chapter 7). The basic idea is that the features we are gathering – in this case, the features of pain – are distinctive of the particular *role*, or *function*, of the entity we are interested in – in this case the role that pain has in a human organism. In other words, to understand what pain is, we must first look at the *job* pain does.

We can now consider applying this method to properties. If we can construct a list of the features taken to be characteristic to properties, then this will be a big help when it comes to assessing the various theories of properties that have been proposed. In particular, we will be looking for the *roles* philosophers have taken to be distinctive of properties. By doing this we will glean insights into the *function* of properties, which will help us in the project of discerning what properties *are*: to find the essence of properties, we need to look for those entities that discharge the jobs of properties.

Of course, as we will see, things might not be so simple in this case though, as a cursory look at the study of properties suggests that properties have a number of *different* – and perhaps incompatible – features. This might tell us that some of these features are not really features of properties at all, or perhaps it may tell us that we need *different kinds* of properties to do all the different jobs that properties are taken to do.

1.4   The Jobs Properties Do

We can take four initial alleged features of properties from the arguments for properties that we have looked at so far. These are:

Properties are things that different objects can have in common We noted that it looks as though we need properties to explain what it is that different objects have in common. For instance, the property of being red is something that fire engines and roses have in common. This is one job that properties have been taken to do, then: be the kinds of things that different objects have in common.

Properties mark genuine similarities In addition to properties being the kinds of things that objects have in common, we also noted that they are able to show how different objects can be similar in a very genuine way. For example, we noted that you and I both have the property of being human. This is a property that we (and many others) share, and it marks something significant about how we are similar. This is another job that properties can do: they can mark genuine similarities as well as similarities.[2]

Properties serve as the semantic values of predicates We also saw that properties can do the job of being the semantic values of predicates. For example, 'the rose is red' is a standard subject–predicate sentence of the form '*a* is F', where 'the rose' (the subject term) refers to an object: the rose. What about the predicate 'is red'? What does this refer to? Not to a single object, as many objects are red; instead it refers to the property of being red.[3]

Properties serve as semantic values of abstract singular terms We noted that most singular terms refer to a single object, but that there are some which do not seem to fit this model, such as 'redness' and 'humility'. Another job that properties can do is to serve as referents of these abstract singular terms; so the property of redness can serve as the referent of 'redness', for example.

These are all jobs that we can take properties to do, and they stem from the core arguments for the existence of properties: they are jobs that, it is claimed, it would be very difficult for any other kind of entity to fulfil. There are also other jobs that some philosophers have proposed for properties, which do not originate directly from the core arguments. We will look at some of these jobs as we progress through the book, so it is worth discussing them briefly here.

Properties ground duplication This is a job that, we might think, follows from the jobs mentioned earlier, which take properties to ground similarities between objects. If two objects that are similar have some properties in common, we might think that two objects that share exactly the same properties are perfect duplicates.

Properties ground the causal powers of objects Many philosophers think that a key job that properties can do is ground the causal powers of objects. In other words, the properties that an object has determine the causal powers that that object has. We might think that it is *because* of certain properties an object has that it has the causal powers it does: it is *because* the table has the property of being solid that I cannot put my fist through it.

As you can see, there are many different features that properties have been taken to have. In particular, we can note that there seems to be both *metaphysical* jobs that properties do (ground similarities, causal powers, and duplication), and *semantic* jobs that properties do (serve as referents for predicates and abstract singular terms). As we will see as we go along, it may be difficult to give a theory of properties that is able to do justice to all of these features. Whether this means that some of the features have to go or whether the theories are no good is a matter that we will discuss as we progress.

The general overarching theme of the book, though, will be that it might be a mistake to think that there is just one kind of entity that can do all of these jobs. In other words, we might find that the best way to think about properties is to take a 'pluralist' approach and keep being open-minded about the idea that there might be different kinds of properties suited to perform different kinds of jobs.

1.5 Definitions and Terminological Notes

The final task of this chapter is to give some definitions and make some terminological notes. As you may well know, debates in philosophy are often made more confusing by the fact that different people sometimes use the same term in different ways, often meaning different things. This is particularly so in debates about properties, where the terms 'universal' and 'nominalism' are perhaps the main offenders. In this final section I will briefly document some of the different uses of some of the terms you might come across, and I will state clearly how I will be using these terms in the present book.

UNIVERSAL A term reserved for a particular kind of entities, which some philosophers identify with properties. Sometimes the noun 'universals' is used to designate what I here mean by 'properties', but, given the influence of Armstrong's theory of universals, it is more accurate to say that universals constitute a particular account of what properties are, 'properties' being the more general and neutral term. Thus, for example, views that deny the existence of universals do not necessarily deny the existence of properties.

REALISM A term sometimes used to describe the view that properties are universals. I will avoid using it in this way in this book, primarily because the term 'realism' is notoriously vague, and also in order to avoid confusion with its applications elsewhere in philosophy, as discussed in Chapter 7.

NOMINALISM Sometimes 'nominalism' is a term used to describe any theory that denies a particular view of properties, namely that properties are *universals*.[4] Included in this bracket, though, are a wide variety of views: trope theory, 'class', 'predicate', 'concept' and 'mereological' nominalism, and 'ostrich' nominalism, to name a few. In this book I will use the term to denote any view that denies that properties constitute a distinct, sui generis ontological class, which I take to be the most natural distinction between theories of properties. So, for the purposes of this book, nominalism equates the denial that properties are universals or tropes.

RELATIONS Properties are usually taken to be picked out by 'one-place' predicates of the form 'is F' – such as 'is red', 'is metallic'. Relations are picked out by predicates that have more than one place, such as two-place predicates like 'is the father of' or 'is to the left of'. Most of what I say about properties also applies to relations, but I will flag moments where this may not necessarily be the case.

OBJECT/PARTICULAR The primary kind of thing that is the bearer of properties. I use the terms 'object' and 'particular' interchangeably throughout the book.

PREDICATE A linguistic construction of the form 'is F' – such as 'is red' and 'is human'. These are often the linguistic entities that are taken to ascribe properties to objects in simple sentences of the form 'x is F' – such as 'the rose is red'. Some views take it that properties are the *semantic values* of predicates.

SINGULAR TERM A term that refers to a single object; the category includes names such as 'Jane Austen' or 'Hillary Clinton' and definite descriptions such as 'the president of the USA' or 'the tallest mountain in the world'. Singular terms take up the position of 'x' in simple sentences of the form 'x is F', and they are the things predicates ascribe properties to.

ABSTRACT SINGULAR TERM A term that takes up the 'x' position in a simple 'x is F' sentence but seems to refer to an entity that exists in more than one place. Some examples are 'redness', 'humanity', and 'electronhood'. Properties are taken by some to serve as the referents of abstract singular terms.

IDENTITY CONDITIONS FOR PROPERTIES Some philosophers[5] complain that properties are suspect entities because there are no clear *identity conditions* for them: that is, there are no clear conditions set out for what makes one property identical to another. Given the variety of views we will examine in this book, such a complaint is not entirely unwarranted, as the controversy over the nature of properties inevitably yields unclarity about the identity conditions for properties. What we can do, though, is show that identity conditions for properties drop out of the various views we will consider, and thus what one takes the identity conditions for properties to be will depend on the view of properties one adopts. We need not get bogged down in details at this point, but here are some brief examples of statements of identity conditions for properties from some of the views we will consider. These will make a handy guide for us to refer back to:

- transcendental universals (Chapter 2): property A = property B if and only if [= iff] the Form of A = the Form of B;
- immanent universals (Chapter 2): property A = property B iff the causal powers of A = the causal powers of B;
- trope theory (Chapter 3): property A = property B iff the class of A tropes = the class of B tropes;
- predicate nominalism (Chapter 5): property A = property B iff the predicate 'is A' and the predicate 'is B' have the same meaning;
- concept nominalism (Chapter 5): property A = property B iff the concept <A> = the concept <B>;
- class nominalism (Chapter 5): property A = property B iff the class of A things = the class of B things;
- mereological nominalism (Chapter 5): property A = property B iff the object A = the object B.

Pluralist theories of different kinds (Chapter 6) will entertain some combinations of these views. On these accounts, the identity claims will be restricted to certain kinds of properties. For instance, a view holding that abundant properties are classes and natural properties are immanent universals will hold that abundant properties have the identity conditions given by class nominalism and natural properties have the identity conditions given by immanent universals.

1.6   Further Reading

We will revisit all of the issues discussed in this chapter as we go through the book, particularly the strength of the reasons for the existence of properties that we derive from the three arguments discussed. The further reading suggested here is thus – primarily – reading designed to give a sense of the shape of the arguments and issues (as opposed to giving a critical discussion, which will be explored later on). As some of the texts mentioned will also be discussed in greater depth later on, one may prefer to continue reading through the rest of the book before returning to explore in some detail the further reading listed here.

To learn more on the structure of the one over many argument, see Armstrong 1978a, Introduction; 1989, chapter 1; and 1997a. See also Moreland 2001, chapter 1 and Rodriguez-Pereyra 2002, chapters 1 and 2 for a different take on the issue. On the reference and quantification arguments, see Lewis 1983, Moreland 2001: Ch. 1 and van Inwagen 2004. Ramsey 1925 is an interesting discussion of the distinction between predicates and singular terms in the context of the distinction between objects and properties. On the causal features of properties, see Shoemaker 1980, and on duplication, see Lewis 1983. On the various roles that properties are given, see Lewis 1983, Oliver 1996, Swoyer 1996, and van Inwagen 2004.

2
Universals

2.1 Introduction

We will begin by looking at perhaps the most famous theory of properties: the theory that properties are *universals*. There are two main views of universals. The first holds that universals are *transcendental* entities – that is, they exist completely separately from the particulars that instantiate them – and the second holds that universals are *immanent*, existing (in some sense) *in* the particulars that instantiate them. The first view is often attributed to Plato and Russell; the second view is often attributed to Aristotle and has been developed extensively by David Armstrong in recent times.

2.2 Transcendental Universals

The theory of transcendental universals has its origins in Plato and was developed in the early twentieth century by Bertrand Russell. We will focus here primarily on the formulations given by Plato and Russell, as they allow us to set up the main proposal and objections nicely. As we will note below, the view has somewhat fallen out of favour since Russell, but directions to more contemporary proposals will be given in the Further Reading section.

2.2.1 *Platonic Forms and the Arguments for Properties*

Plato and Russell use the one over many argument that we reviewed in the last chapter to argue for the existence of transcendental universals: many different particular things, whether they be red objects, just acts, or human beings, seem to have the same nature. How best to explain this? One answer is that they share something: that there is some property such as *redness*, *justice* or *humanity* that is shared by all of the objects, acts and beings in question. One way to find out what these properties or natures are is to try to abstract each one of them from the various particular features of the objects that share that property – in other words, to try to find out precisely what it is that all just actions have that *makes them* just acts. So, for example, we might take two examples of just actions and abstract away from features such as the times at which they were performed, the identity of their particular agents, the places in which they occurred, and so forth, until we find the thing they seemingly share in virtue of which they are just. *This* feature – whatever it may be – will be *justice itself*. These 'pure essences' are what Plato called 'Forms', the thought being that all just acts, for example, 'participate' in the form of *justice*.

We can note that the Forms can also be used to satisfy the demands of the reference argument. Here are, once again, our examples:

(1)   Red resembles orange more than it resembles blue.
(2)   Red is a colour.
(3)   Humility is a virtue.
(4)   Redness is a sign of ripeness.

The transcendental view has a very simple answer to the question of what the particular referents are for, for example, 'red', 'orange', 'blue' and 'humility': each one refers to a single entity, respectively the Form of red, the Form of orange, the Form of blue and the Form of humility. The view can also account for the relations between properties that these sentences register, in that the sentences can be said to be making reference to relations *between* the Forms in question. So (1) can be read as saying that the Form of red resembles the Form of orange more than it resembles the Form of blue.

2.2.2   Universals as Abstract

The Forms can be thought to be abstract in the sense that they do not exist in space and time. As Russell writes:

> The [Form] *justice* is not identical with anything that is just: it is something other than particular things, which particular things partake of. Not being particular, it cannot exist itself in the world of sense. Moreover, it is not fleeting or change-able like the things of sense: it is eternally itself, immutable and indestructible. (Russell 1967: 52/1997: 45)

A number of things are going on in this passage. First of all, we have the idea that a Form is distinct from any of the particular things that participate in it: thus justice (*qua* Form) is distinct from each of the individual just acts. Russell then claims that the Form is not a particular, and seemingly that, as only particulars exist in time and space, the Form does not exist in this realm. This thought is substantiated by the idea that the Forms (like the Form of justice) are unchanging and indestructible, unlike particular entities existing in time and space. What we end up with, then, is the sensible world of time and space, separated from the abstract realm of the Forms.

It is worth making a couple of points though, to fill some of the gaps in the reasoning. Firstly, it is worth noting that 'particular', in Russell's usage, is *defined* as an entity 'given in sensation', whereas a universal is something that 'may be shared by many particulars'. Without these provisions, the claim that the Form of, say, justice, is not a particular might look a bit odd; for there is only *one* Form of justice. Despite this, though, in Russell's and in Plato's terms it is not a par-ticular because, they claim, it is not given to us in sensation and it is shared by many things that are.

One might also think the claim that we do not perceive universals to be a bit strange; for do we not see red and white, for example, around us all the time? Notice, though, that the claim is not that we fail to perceive the properties that objects have; the claim is not that we cannot see the whiteness of a piece of paper, for example. But what we see is a *particular* object's whiteness, not the *Form* of whiteness, which is shared by all white things. So Plato and Russell are not denying that we perceive *particular cases* of whiteness and redness; what they are denying is that we perceive *whiteness* and *redness* themselves: these must be abstracted from all of the individual perceptions of particulars. The idea is, then, that we cannot perceive the Forms themselves through sense perception; all that we can ever grasp through perception is the particular objects' participation in those Forms.

The claim that whiteness is immutable and indestructible comes from the thought that, even if I add colour to the particular piece of paper to change it from white to red, *whiteness itself* (*qua* Form) remains unchanged, despite the addition of colour to that particular piece of paper. Likewise, if I destroy the paper, that particular instance of whiteness is destroyed, but *whiteness itself* (qua Form) remains in existence; and, intuitively, this would be the case even if *all* white particulars were destroyed.

Both Plato and Russell hold that universals – conceived of as Forms – do not exist in the same way as particular objects like tables and chairs. Plato held that they exist in a 'more real' sense, as the Forms constituted the 'true reality' of which the world of sense is a pale imitation.[1] Russell also accepts that there are differences in the status of universals and particulars, though he does not hold, with Plato, that one is 'more real' than the other. In fact he introduces a new term to capture the status of universals: he says that they 'subsist' or have 'being'. This sets them in contrast with the things that *exist*, which are particular spatiotemporal objects. He says:

> The world of being is unchangeable, rigid, exact, delightful to the mathematician, the logician, the builder of metaphysical systems, and all who love perfection more than life. The world of existence is fleeting, vague, without sharp boundaries, without any clear plan or arrangement, but it contains all thoughts and feelings, all data of sense, and all physical objects, everything that can do either good or harm, everything that makes any difference to the value of life and the world. (Russell 1967: 57/1997: 50)

These differences between the realm of universals and the realm of particulars cause Russell to hold that we must say that items in one have *being*, while items in the other *exist*. However, dividing things up in this way can cause a lot of problems.[2] Perhaps a better way to put the distinction is to use more contemporary devices and hold that items in both realms exist, but that they exist in different ways. In particular, we might say that items in the realm of universals exist *abstractly*, whereas items in the realm of particulars exist *concretely*. Roughly speaking, this distinction maps onto the distinction Russell makes, but it holds that all the items in question *exist*, only they do so in different senses. Concrete objects are those that exist in space and time; feature in causal relations; undergo change; and can – in principle – be perceived by the senses. Abstract objects, on the other hand, exist timelessly, have no particular spatial location, do not feature in causal relations and cannot be perceived by the senses.

One thing that it is important to note in relation to this distinction – and a point Russell insists on – is that universals are *not* dependent on minds for their existence. Things that exist abstractly exist mind-independently, and this includes universals. There is a sense in which this should be immediately apparent from Russell's quotation above; for minds (and the ideas contained within them) exist in the concrete realm, and minds – like everything else in this realm – are subject to change and destruction, whereas universals, being abstract, are eternal and immutable. This means that universals existed long before any minds were around to apprehend them, and would continue to exist were all minds destroyed. The example Russell uses to illustrate this is the example of the relation 'to the north of', as featured for example in the claim that Edinburgh is to the north of London. The fact that Edinburgh is to the north of London, Russell claims, along with the universal it contains, is completely mind-independent:

> When we come to know that Edinburgh is to the north of London, we come to know something which has to do only with Edinburgh and London: we do not cause the truth of proposition by coming to know it, on the contrary we merely apprehend a fact which was there before we know it. The part

of the earth's surface where Edinburgh stands would be north of the part where London stands, even if there were no human being to know about north and south, and even if there were no minds at all in the universe . . . But this fact involves the relation 'north of', which is a universal; and it would be impossible for the whole fact to involve nothing mental if the relation 'north of', which is a constituent part of the fact, did involve anything mental. (Russell 1967: 56/1997: 49)[3]

However, as Russell notices, there is a difficulty here, in that the relation 'to the north of' seems to exist 'nowhere and nowhen': it does not seem to exist in London or in Edinburgh, nor does it exist at any particular time. Russell concludes that it is neither mental nor physical – nor concrete at all, but abstract.

Notice, also, that this view can make sense of the idea that there are *uninstantiated* properties – that is, properties that have never been (and perhaps will never be) instantiated by any particular object. For instance, take the property of being perfectly circular. This is a property that is not (and has not) been instantiated, yet we may want to say that there is such a property – especially if we take the reference argument (noted above) to have some force. The transcendental view can account for perfect circularity, as, even though there are no *particulars* that participate in it, there is nevertheless a Form of perfect circularity, which exists abstractly. This Form – or universal – can thus be retained as the referent of the phrase 'is perfectly circular'; and, as it is abstract, it does not matter that it has not been instantiated by any particular.

Perhaps the more important reason for positing uninstantiated universals, however, has to do with the notion of perfection alluded to by Russell in the quotation above. Plato himself noted that, in the world of sense, there are no perfect instantiations of universals. For example, no particular object is perfectly circular and no person or action is perfectly just: they are all defective in some sense. However, the thought goes, we are still able to contemplate and discuss the notion of perfect circularity or perfect justice (in geometry and in moral philosophy, for example), so how do we explain these notions if we have no particular examples to attach them to? One answer is given by the transcendental view: there is perfect circularity and perfect justice; they are to be found, respectively, in the Forms of circularity and justice; and what we try to do in our investigations is get to the nature of the Forms. The fact that we have no particular examples of perfection of these sorts does not mean that there is no such thing, for in each case we can appeal to the Form as the root of the idea of perfection.

2.2.3   The Relation between Particulars and Universals

The relation between particulars and universals is puzzling on the transcendent view. They are clearly related, as particular objects have properties; but an object's having a property seems to express some sort of relation between a particular object, which exists spatiotemporally, and an abstract non-spatiotemporal Form. What could this relation be? So far we have been operating with the idea that, when particulars exhibit a certain property, they 'participate' in the Form in question. For instance, a white sheet of paper *participates* in the Form (universal) *whiteness*. But what exactly does it mean for an object to participate in a Form?

Taken literally, the notion of participation (or 'partaking', as Russell puts it) implies that the relation between particulars and universals involves the particulars 'taking part in' the universal. That is, if a white piece of paper participates in the Form of whiteness, then it is in some sense a *part of* that Form – just like, if I participate in a game of football, I am in a sense a *part of* that game. This would seem to be an odd picture though, given the clear ontological differences between particulars and universals. For one thing, it would mean that all particulars that partake in a universal are *parts of* that universal, but, given that particulars are concrete and universals abstract, this would mean that an abstract object would have concrete parts, which seems mistaken. Moreover, as Armstrong (1978a: 66) points out, taking the relation in this way would seem to obstruct one of the main points of introducing universals in the first place, which was to explain commonalities between particulars. This is because, on this account, it looks as though each white particular constitutes a *different* part of the Form *whiteness*; but, if each particular constitutes a different part, then there is no single thing that they all share in common, for they are, each, numerically different parts of the Form.[4] We would now need something *further*, something to explain what it is that unifies the white particulars – which, if Forms are understood in this way, cannot be the Form of whiteness itself; so the very point of introducing the Form seems to be undermined.

A different way of accounting for the relation, and one suggested by Plato, is to hold that particulars *resemble* the Form. This is suggested when the characters of Socrates and Glaucon talk about the relation between a particular bed, made by a carpenter, and the form of bed:

> 'And what about the carpenter? Didn't you agree that what he produces is not the Form of bed, which according to us is what a bed really is, but a particular bed?'
> 'I did.'
> 'If, then, what he makes is not "what a bed really is", his product is not "what is", but something which *resembles* "what is" without *being it*. And anyone who says that the products of the carpenter or any other craftsman are ultimately real can hardly be telling the truth, can he?' (*Republic*, 597a)

On this account, a particular bed participates in the Form of bed by *resembling* the form.[5] Plato does not give a great deal of explanation of how this is to work, but some simple considerations show that the suggestion is not particularly promising. Without any guidance of the *sense* in which the form and the particular are supposed to resemble each other, it is actually quite hard to see how there could be *any* resemblance between the two. The Form, after all, is abstract, immutable, indestructible and insensible, whereas the bed is concrete, changeable, destructible and sensible. The *ontological* differences between Forms and particulars in general seem to make it very difficult to see how a particular could resemble a Form.[6]

Things are not helped if we say that the resemblance is found in the natures of the particular and the universal themselves. For instance, we might say that white particulars resemble the Form of whiteness because the Form, like the particulars, is white. This may then account for the resemblance: the particulars and the Form are all white. However, to take this line is to walk straight into what is known as the third man regress or the third man argument.[7] In its simplest form, the argument suggests that taking this line – holding that the form of whiteness is itself white – leads to new (and never-ending) one over many problems. Remember that one of the main points of introducing the Form of whiteness was to provide unity to all the particular white things: all of these things were joined in nature by their participation in the Form of whiteness. But now suppose that the Form of whiteness is itself white. Now we have a new collection of things that need unifying: all of the particular white things *and* the white Form of whiteness. So now the unity of *this* collection needs to be accounted for. One thing we might do is introduce a *new* Form of whiteness – $Form_{w2}$ – which binds together the particular white things and the old Form of whiteness – $Form_{w1}$. But then the initial question arises once again: how do we account for the resemblance between (1) the collection of particular white things, (2) whiteness $Form_{w1}$ and (3) whiteness $Form_{w2}$? Is it that whiteness $Form_{w2}$ is also white? If we say this, though, then we will need a new Form of whiteness – $Form_{w3}$ – to bind all of these together, and so on ad infinitum.

The third man regress thus suggests that we cannot say that the Forms themselves participate in themselves. That is, the Form of whiteness, for example, cannot participate in the Form of whiteness: it cannot itself be white. This causes a further problem for the account of participation as resemblance: not only is there the vast difference in ontological status between particulars and the Form, but there cannot be any resemblance on the basis of *the Form itself*. With these options exhausted, it is hard to see how the resemblance account can survive.

A further problem for the transcendental view's ability to account for the relation between particulars and universals is brought out by Armstrong's 'relation regress'. As we will see, this regress threatens almost every theory of properties that we will come across, so it may not identify a problem specific to transcendental universals; but it is a problem all the same. The regress works whether we take the relation to be one of *participation* (in the sense of 'partaking') or one of *resemblance*.

Let us use resemblance as an example. The resemblance account holds that the relation between a particular and a universal is one of *resemblance*: a particular (say, a piece of paper) has a property (say, whiteness) if it resembles the appropriate universal (the Form of whiteness). It is important to note – as Russell does – that this analysis is supposed to hold for *both* monadic properties *and* relations (such as 'to the north of'). Thus all relations, as well as all properties, must be accounted for in terms of their resemblance to the relevant universal. But now note, as again Russell himself famously emphasises, that *resemblance* is *itself* a relation, and as such it must be accounted for in terms of a universal, the Form of resemblance.[8] Now we have a bit of a problem: our analysis of the possession of all properties and relations by particulars – that they resemble the appropriate universal – *itself* includes a relation, *resemblance*. But how do we account for *this* relation, the relation of resemblance? If we say that the relation of resemblance is instantiated whenever the particular instance of the relation of resemblance resembles the Form of resemblance, then our analysis is circular: it uses the relation of resemblance to analyse the relation of resemblance, which cannot be correct.

If we take it one way, circularity beckons. But, if we take it the other way, we seem to be led into a regress. Consider again *resemblance*, a relation that holds between a particular and a universal. The rose *resembles* the universal *redness*. We can write the pair {rose, redness},[9] and say that {rose, redness} instantiates the relation *resemblance*. How do we do this? To instantiate a relation is, for that particular instance of the relation, to resemble the corresponding universal; so we will have to say that {rose, redness} *resembles* the universal *resemblance*. But notice that, in order to do this, we have to have a new pair, consisting of the pair of the rose and redness on the one hand, and the universal of resemblance on the other – {{rose, redness}, resemblance} – which instantiates the relation *resemblance* by resembling the universal *resemblance*. However, if we are to avoid circularity, we cannot have it that this resemblance universal is the same as the resemblance universal in the new pair; so we have to hold that this new

Form of resemblance is of a different level from (or of a 'higher order' than) the initial Form of resemblance. To point this out, we will mark it as resemblance$_2$. But notice that the problem does not end here, because, in order to say that the new pair instantiates the relation of resemblance, we have to say that it resembles the universal resemblance$_2$. But again, on pain of circularity, in order to be able to say *this*, we now need a new pair {{{rose, redness}, resemblance}, resemblance$_2$}, which instantiates the resemblance relation by resembling an even higher-order universal, *resemblance$_3$*. But this will yield a *further* pair, {{{{rose, redness}, resemblance}, resemblance$_2$}, resemblance$_3$} which will need to resemble the even higher-order universal *resemblance$_4$* – and so on, ad infinitum.

If we try to account for the relation between a particular and a universal in terms of resemblance, we are left with a dilemma: we'll have either a circular analysis or one that leads to an infinite regress. In neither case, it seems, do we end up with a satisfactory grip on the relation between a particular and a universal. Moreover, because participation is also a relation, the very same dilemma will occur in that case too.

What, then, can we say about the relation between a particular and a universal on this view? One option is to hold, with Cook Wilson (1926), that the relation is primitive: that there is no substantive explanation forthcoming. While this sounds immensely dissatisfying, we will see that almost every view of properties has to take something as primitive, and usually that is precisely the relation between object and property. In this sense, while the view leaves one dissatisfied, it does not leave one any worse off than most other theories of properties. This issue is also picked up by David Lewis and David Armstrong, and we will examine it in greater detail as we progress; but let us have a quick think about it now.

2.2.4   Taking Things as Primitive

To take something to be 'primitive' is to hold that there is no explanation of its nature forthcoming. Moreover, this lack of explanation is not simply due to our inability to give an account at the present time while we hope that the situation will change in the future; it is rather the case that the item in question has *in principle* no explanation. This is what occurs with the relation between particular and universal described above: there is no way to explain it. Hence, short of denying the existence of the relation, we can say that the relation is primitive – that it has no explanation. As we will see, pretty much every theory has to take some thing(s) to be primitive, and indeed this should not be too surprising: as Wittgenstein famously said (though in a different context), 'explanations come to an end somewhere' (Wittgenstein 1953: §1 – almost repeating word for word Aristotle's no less famous imperative *anankē stēnai*, 'we must stop somewhere'). In other words, every theory needs some building blocks to start from, which can then be used to explain other things. If everything were explained in terms of something else while we would not have primitive notions, we would have either circular explanations or infinite chains of explanations – which is, arguably, not a good situation to be in. So primitive notions are perhaps unavoidable. But this is not to say that they should be allowed to proliferate or multiply; in fact they should be minimised. As Lewis puts it:

> The object of analysis is to reduce our burden of primitive notions, and to make tacit understanding explicit – not to bootstrap ourselves into understanding what we didn't understand at all beforehand. (Lewis 1986b: 154)

Perhaps, then, we could think of analysis in the following way. Before we begin analysing something, we have no explanations; so, in a sense, everything we are looking at is primitive. As we proceed through our project of analysis we begin to explain things, and so gradually we reduce the number of unexplained things. But there may be a point where explanation gives out, so to speak, and where we cannot give any further explanation of something. In this case – as in the case of the relation between particular and universal above – we have to take the thing in question as primitive. But it should be clear that more powerful theories will be theories that leave fewer things as primitives, as they will be able to explain more things – hence they will have greater explanatory power. This is why, while we may accept that all theories have to take some things as primitives, the number of primitives a theory takes should better be as low as possible. This is one dimension along which theories can be compared.[10]

2.2.5   Summary

According to the transcendental view of universals, properties are identified with universals, which exist abstractly, outside of space and time. Uninstantiated properties are taken to be possible, and the relation between particular and universal is taken to be primitive. As we have seen, this view is subject to two serious regress problems. It also suffers when we attempt to account for the idea that properties ground the causal powers of objects; for properties themselves, on this view – by definition – exist outside of the causal realm of space and time. Granted, we might think that particular instantiations of a property in an object might make for some causal powers, but this leaves the properties themselves inert. For these reasons, and perhaps also for the metaphysical peculiarities of the view, transcendental universals have received less attention than immanent universals in contemporary debates.[11] This may seem a little unfair, particularly as many views share problems of similar magnitude, as we will see. We will return to transcendental universals in Chapter 5 in our discussion of the properties posited by predicate/ concept nominalism, but we will now turn to discuss immanent universals, which will be the view of universals that we will primarily work with in the rest of the book.

2.3   Immanent Universals

The second view of universals that we will examine in this chapter takes them not to be separate from the particulars that instantiate them, but rather *immanent* in them. By far the most influential and extensively developed proposal along these lines is that given by David Armstrong. While the thesis of immanent universals is a general one and can be separated from Armstrong's specific thesis, we will focus primarily on Armstrong's development of the idea and will note the points where others may depart.

It is fair to say that David Armstrong is the contemporary philosopher who has most substantially influenced debates about properties in the twentieth and twenty-first centuries. His arguments for the theory of 'immanent universals', along with his arguments against other views, form the backbone of the subject in recent times, as should be clear from the presence of his work in every chapter of this book. In this section we will focus on his positive view that we should posit two basic categories of being, particulars and universals, and that universals are 'immanent' in the particulars that possess them. We will also, towards the end of the chapter, review Armstrong's general attitude of 'a posteriori realism' about universals, which dictates – for him – what universals we ought to posit.

2.3.1 The Relation between Particulars and Universals

The first issue to consider, though, is how Armstrong conceives of universals and how he conceives of the relation between particulars and universals. Armstrong rejects the view of Plato and Russell that universals exist in a different realm from particulars; he holds instead that universals exist 'in' the particulars that have them. A metaphor that Armstrong uses in thinking of particulars imagines them like layer cakes: the universals that the particular possesses would be the layers in the cake. Seen in this way, the universals literally are components of the particular that possesses them, though Armstrong does not think that particulars are simply reducible to the universals in their composition.

As we have seen, trying to account for the *relation* between universal and particular is a difficult task. On the transcendental view, universals and particulars are taken to be separate entities and thus need to be related, resemblance and participation being two candidates. As we saw, these two proposals met with severe difficulties. However, Armstrong notes, *any* view which holds that universals and particulars need to be related will be subject to the same problems. Even if we just try to say, innocently, that particulars *instantiate* universals, we will run into the very same trouble as we saw above with resemblance. This is because, if instantiation is a relation, then it will need to be shown how a universal and a particular instantiate the relation of instantiation, which will lead to the very same regress or circularity as presented above.

Armstrong chooses to take a different tack. He denies, firstly, that universal and particular are distinct in the way in which the transcendental view holds them to be, and, secondly, that they are related. Let us take the first claim. The transcendental view holds that universals and particulars are very different kinds of entity and exist independently of each other. In particular, it may be said that universals can be completely free of the particulars that instantiate them, existing as they do in the abstract realm, and also potentially uninstantiated. At the other extreme is the view that particulars and universals are not distinct, because the former are reducible to the latter. This view, commonly called 'the bundle theory' of particulars, holds that particulars are nothing over and above a bundle of universals, and hence objects are nothing but a collection of properties. Armstrong rejects both of these pictures and holds that universals and particulars are distinct kinds of things, neither being reducible to the other; they are rather co-dependent – that is, each depends for its existence on the other.

This is encapsulated in two principles:

(1) THE PRINCIPLE OF INSTANTIATION: For each N-adic universal, U, there exist at least N particulars such that they are U;

(2) THE PRINCIPLE OF THE REJECTION OF BARE PARTICULARS: For each particular, x, there exists at least one universal, U, such that x is U.[12]

(1) ties the existence of universals to the existence of particulars, for it denies the existence of uninstantiated universals: every universal must (at one time or another) be instantiated by some particular. (2) ties the existence of particulars to the existence of universals, for it denies the possibility of a particular existing without it having some universal. In this way universals and particulars are inseparable; neither can exist without the other.

Universal and particular are, then, inseparable on Armstrong's view; but are they related? As strange as it might seem, Armstrong says no, holding that his view is a *non-relational immanent realism*. It is non-relational because he denies that, when we say that a particular instantiates a universal, this means that there is a relation between the two. Instead he holds that we should think in terms of *states of affairs*:

> talking about states of affairs is a simpler and more perspicuous way of talking than talking about instantiation. The *fundamental tie*, or *nexus*, in a Universals theory is nothing but the bringing together of particulars and universals in states of affairs (Armstrong 1989: 110)

For Armstrong, universals and particulars are united in states of affairs. We can think of a state of affairs as a fusion between a universal and a particular. The sky's being blue, for example, is a state of affairs, as is the state of affairs of my being human. Armstrong's states of affairs are particular ways in which the world is; and he takes these states of affairs – these ways the world is – to be the most basic constituents of reality: the world is composed of various states of affairs. Taking states of affairs to be basic is important for our purposes, as it allows us to define the notions of universals and particulars in terms of them: universals and particulars are constituents of states of affairs. This, for Armstrong, explains the tie between universals and particulars: they come together not through some relation obtaining between them, but by virtue of being fused together as constituents of states of affairs.

This is why, for Armstrong, the question of whether particulars are more basic than universals (or vice versa) is somewhat ill formed. The view that takes particulars to be more basic must allow for the possibility of 'bare particulars' – that is, we must be able to make sense of the idea that particulars can exist independently of all the universals they might contain.[13] Once we have this idea up and running, we can say that particulars are able to be the sort of thing that would bind together all of their universals, as they provide something other than those universals to bind them all together.

Alternatively, if we take universals to be more basic than particulars and hold that particulars are merely bundles of universals, then we must be able to understand universals as existing independently of particulars and only forming particulars when they come together in such bundles. On Armstrong's view, though, each of these options represents an impossibility. For him, as we have seen, universals and particulars are *co-dependent*; neither can exist without the other. Thus the question of which is more basic, or which depends on the other, is removed from consideration: they either exist together or not at all. In this way Armstrong cancels the debate between those who view particulars as underlying substances and those who view them as bundles of properties; for neither position can get off the ground if we suppose that universals and particulars are as utterly co-dependent as Armstrong thinks they are.

One might wonder whether this account that Armstrong gives is really much different from the one in which the instantiation relation is primitive: on the one hand we accept that we cannot both explain a relation and take it to be primitive, and on the other we end up denying that there is such a relation after all! Indeed, as Lewis (1983), Devitt (1980: 437/1997: 98), Ehring (2011: 127–8) and Maurin (2010) have suggested, the picture Armstrong ends up with is really no less mysterious than the view that one would have if one were to take the relation to be primitive. For all the talk of fundamental ties and states of affairs, it seems that we are no closer to a substantive understanding of what it is for an object to have a property. For this reason, we will treat Armstrong's account as a theoretical cost to bear akin to taking a relation as primitive. While no theory seems to be able to avoid such a move, it is still important to identify the point at which the move is made.

Connected to this issue is Armstrong's thought that universals are – in some sense – *parts* of the particulars that instantiate them:

> We can think of a thing's properties as constituents of the thing and think of the properties as universals . . . properties as universals as part of the internal structure of things. (Armstrong 1989: 77)

If universals are thought of as somehow parts of the particulars that instantiate them, then this further strengthens the intimate connection between particulars and universals, and further throws into doubt the coherence of supposing them to be separable. For example, one might think that it is the nature of a part that its existence *qua* part is inextricably tied to that of the whole that it is a part of. If the whole did not exist, then the part would not exist *as a* part. Likewise, the existence of a whole is closely tied to the existence of its parts: remove all of its parts and the whole itself ceases to exist.

If we take universals to be parts of particulars, though, some interesting questions arise. For instance, if we are taking particulars to be concrete objects, existing at a particular point in space and time, then normally we can take parts of those objects to have particular spatiotemporal locations. Thus we can locate a table at a particular point, and we can also locate its parts, such as its legs and its top, at particular points. But it seems to be otherwise with universals: while we can locate the table's legs at particular points, it does not look as though we can locate the table's brownness or woodenness at particular points too. These seem to be very different things from the table's legs or top. Considerations such as this one have led some, such as David Lewis and Keith Campbell, to consider Armstrong's universals as being *non-spatiotemporal* parts of objects:

> A universal is supposed to be wholly present wherever it is instantiated. It is a constituent part (though not a spatiotemporal part) of each particular that has it. (Lewis 1983: 344/1997: 190)
>
> [Armstrong's view] requires us to acknowledge that there can be parts other than spatio-temporal parts. (Campbell 1990: 39)

This interpretation may cause some problems though, particularly when we consider that universals are supposed to ground the *causal powers* of objects. As we noted earlier when examining transcendental universals, if universals are taken to exist outside of space and time, then, on the assumption that causal interactions happen *within* space–time, universals seemingly cannot feature in causal interactions. However, for those like Armstrong, who want universals to ground the causal powers of objects, this looks like a bad result. Note also that, at least on Lewis's interpretation, it is not only universals that are taken to exist non-spatiotemporally, but also particular instantiations of them. Thus, for example, the woodenness of the table would be a non-spatiotemporal part of the table on this view; but then it seems difficult to see how the woodenness of the table could feature in the many causal interactions we take it to feature in.

However, as Ted Sider (1995) notes, there is an alternative interpretation available to Armstrong here. This is to accept that we cannot locate the particular part of the table that is its woodenness and to hold instead that the woodenness of the table is located where the whole table itself is located. In the same way, my humanity cannot be located in just my little finger or my big toe, rather it must be considered to be wherever I myself am as a whole. On this interpretation, we do not understand universals to be parts of particulars in the same way in which we understand the legs of the table to be parts of the table; nonetheless universals are still taken to have spatiotemporal location. We can note that, on this view, it is not just particular instantiations of a universal that will have a spatiotemporal location, but also the universal as a whole. The universal will be spatiotemporally located in *all* the places where it is instantiated. Thus the universal woodenness, for example, will exist at all the places where woodenness is instantiated, namely all the wooden objects.

It is important to note that such a view must be able to make sense of the idea of *co-location*. On this view, a single unit of space–time will play host to a number of different entities. For example, take again the table. In one single unit of space–time we will have the table, but we will also have the universals that the table instantiates, namely its woodenness and its brownness, to name just a couple. These three things will all occupy the exact same unit of space-time; hence it is important that this interpretation takes on board the idea that more than one thing can exist at the same place at the same time. Granted, this idea may seem intuitively suspect, but we can note that *many* of the things we say about universals will seem intuitively suspect because – as Lewis

(1983) points out – many of our intuitions in this area spring from considerations about *whole objects*, not properties. For instance, it seems intuitively difficult to take on board the idea that a single thing can exist in several places at once, but this is a very basic tenet of Armstrong's theory of universals. It is difficult to make sense of this intuitively, because our intuitions are tailored for whole objects, of which, naturally, it seems impossible to think that they could exist in several places at once. However, we have to overcome this difficulty if we are to admit of universals as a genuine class of being. Likewise, it may be difficult to grasp intuitively the idea that more than one thing can exist in the same place at the same time; but, once we acknowledge that we are not talking here about two *objects* existing in the same place at the same time but about a combination of objects and universals, then the intuitive prohibition should be lifted.

This second interpretation seems to fit better with Armstrong's own concerns about the ability of universals to ground the causal powers of objects, though he himself in more recent work has tried to distance himself somewhat from the issue:

> Talk of locating universals in space–time . . . emerges as a crude way of speaking. Space–time is not a box into which universals are put. Universals are constituents of states of affairs. Space–time is a conjunction of states of affairs. In that sense universals are 'in' space–time. But they are in it as helping to constitute it. (Armstrong 1989: 99)

Armstrong's thought here seems to be that there is something backward about the way the initial question – whether universals exist in space–time – is formed. The way the question is formed seems to suggest that space–time is something *independent* of universals, something into which we then need to see if universals fit. However, equipped with his notion of states of affairs, Armstrong turns the issue on its head. He suggests that states of affairs are *what constitutes space–time itself*, and, as we have seen, universals are constituents of states of affairs. As a result, universals cannot but fit into space–time, not because they need to be fitted into it somehow, but rather because they are constituents of it. This is a somewhat controversial position, though, and perhaps the friend of Armstrong's universals can be left to choose, from the available options we have outlined for accommodating universals in space–time, the one they prefer.

We have now examined the central foundations of Armstrong's theory of immanent universals: we have established the connection between universals and particulars and explained how it differs from the connection posited by the theory of transcendental universals. However, this only really constitutes one half of Armstrong's view. We will now go on to explore the second half, which is heavily coloured by Armstrong's metaphysics in general. As we will see, this leads to some controversial results, though it is worth bearing in mind that the aspects we have looked at so far regarding the relation (or lack thereof) between immanent universals and particulars are somewhat detachable from these further aspects (but this is something we will explore in more detail in the summary of this chapter, and also later in the book, in Chapter 6).

2.3.2 Armstrong's Metaphysical Picture

Armstrong's metaphysics is very different from that advocated by Plato and Russell. His view of existence is encapsulated by what he calls 'the Eleatic principle':

> *Eleatic principle*: Everything that exists makes a difference to the causal powers of something. (Armstrong 1997b: 41)[14]

The main rationale behind Armstrong's making this statement is that Armstrong identifies himself as a *naturalist* and, although this can mean many different things, he thinks, broadly, that the sciences should be used as the sole guide in the question of what exists. As a result, he is sceptical of the idea that there exist 'abstract' objects in the sense advocated by Plato and Russell. This – in one sense – places a limit on the *kinds* of universals that can exist for Armstrong: only universals that are part of the push and pull of causal interaction pass muster.

This has implications for other cases too. Because he thinks that we can only find out what universals exist through a posteriori scientific method, he denies that we can discover the existence of universals through a priori reasoning. This is encapsulated in the exclusion principle:

> *Exclusion principle*: If it can be proved *a priori* that a thing falls under a certain universal, then there is no such universal. (1978b: 11)

One casualty of this principle is the thought that all things have the property of being identical to themselves. Because this is established purely through a priori reasoning, Armstrong holds that there can be no such universal: universals are solely accounted for through a posteriori methods. Moreover, as he identifies properties with universals, there can be no such property either.

2.3.3 Disjunctive, Negative and Conjunctive Universals

The Eleatic principle and the exclusion principle also have some bite when it comes to considering whether negative and disjunctive universals should be allowed, though they do not rule out conjunctive universals. Let us take disjunctive universals first. These would be universals that consisted of the disjunction of two universals, such as being metallic and being negatively charged. The disjunctive universal would be the universal of being negatively charged or metallic. Armstrong rejects the possibility of disjunctive universals of this kind, and he does so on two central grounds. The first stems from the Eleatic principle, which states that, for something to exist, it needs to make a difference to the causal powers of something. We can note that being negatively charged and being metallic seem to pass this test if they are considered independently: the things that are negatively charged have certain causal powers in virtue of being negatively charged, and the things that are metallic seem to have certain causal powers in virtue of being metallic. Now if the disjunctive universal of being negatively charged or metallic were to exist, this would be instantiated by the negatively charged things and the metallic things too, but would it add anything to their causal powers? For instance, would being negatively charged or metallic add anything to the causal powers of a negatively charged thing? Armstrong suggests not: the causal powers here are provided by the thing's being negatively charged, and its being negatively charged or metallic adds nothing to its causal powers. Hence disjunctive universals would not withstand the Eleatic principle and in consequence are rejected.

The second reason has to do with the idea that universals ground genuine similarities between objects. Consider again the prospective universal of being negatively charged or metallic. While we can note that all the negatively charged things will exhibit some genuine similarity and all the metallic things will exhibit some genuine similarity, it will not be the case that all negatively charged things and all metallic things will be genuinely similar. For example, an electron and the Eiffel Tower do not seem to exhibit many genuine similarities; yet, if the disjunctive universal of being negatively charged or metallic is admitted, then they will both instantiate the same universal. This, however, runs contrary to the nature of universals as Armstrong understands them, and thus disjunctive universals must be dismissed.

Two parallel concerns move Armstrong to reject the possibility of negative universals. These would be universals prefaced by a negation operator, such as the universal of not being negatively charged, or the universal of not being metallic. First, consider again the Eleatic principle. For negative universals to be admitted, it would need to be shown that they make a difference to the causal powers of things. But now consider the prospective universal of not being metallic. Paper is the sort of thing that would possess this universal; but would it make a difference to the causal powers of paper? Armstrong thinks not, holding that

> It is a strange idea that lacks or absences do any causing. It is natural to say that a thing acts in virtue of its positive factors alone. This suggests that absences of universals are not universals. (Armstrong 1989: 83)

This issue is somewhat more contentious than the parallel case of disjunctive universals, but we can perhaps offer something in support of Armstrong. Consider again the property of not being metallic. We might think that this grounds some causal powers that paper has, for example its ability to serve as an insulator instead of a conductor. However, while we may *talk* as though it is the paper's not being metallic that gives it this power, it is plausible that its ability to serve as an insulator is *better* explained by the positive universals that the paper instantiates. The claim that Armstrong will push here is that in *all* cases where it looks as though we must admit negative universals to do some causal work, that very work will actually be done by familiar positive universals.

The second reason for rejecting negative universals is a bit more straightforward. Once again, it concerns the ability of universals to ground objective similarities. While the positive universal of being metallic seems to ground objective similarities between the things that instantiate it, it does not seem to be the case that all the things that are not metallic exhibit genuine similarities: the things that are not metallic form an incredibly diverse category. As universals are supposed to ground genuine similarities, negative universals – if admitted – would violate this constraint, and thus there are grounds to reject them as genuine universals.

Things are somewhat different with conjunctive universals, though. An example of a conjunctive universal would be the universal of being liquid and metallic. These survive the tests of genuine similarity and capacity to ground causal powers. In the case of genuine similarity, there will be something significant that all things that instantiate a conjunctive universal share, namely the two universals that compose it. For instance, all things that have the conjunctive universal of being liquid and metallic will instantiate the universal of being liquid and the universal of being metallic. In the case of causal powers, it may well be that the possession of two universals simultaneously imbues a thing with more causal powers than if it just possessed one or the other alone. For example, mercury's being metallic and liquid yields mercury different causal powers from those of something that is only metallic or only liquid.

2.3.4   *Structural Universals*

Conjunctive universals are not the only kinds of complex universals that Armstrong considers. Another kind are structural universals; that is, complex universals that consist of a very specific structure of simpler universals. An example of this kind of universal is methane, given by David Lewis:

> Example: suppose we have monadic universals *carbon* and *hydrogen*, instantiated by atoms of those elements; and a dyadic universal *bonded*, instantiated by pairs of atoms between which there is a covalent bond . . . Then we have, for instance, a structural universal *methane*, which is instantiated by methane molecules. It involves the three previously mentioned universals as follows: necessarily, something instantiates *methane* if and only if it is divisible into five spatial parts c, h_1, h_2, h_3, h_4 such that c instantiates *carbon*, each of the h's instantiate *hydrogen*, and each of the c-h pairs instantiates *bonded*. (Lewis 1986a: 27)

So, supposing that we take carbon and hydrogen to be simple monadic universals, we can determine a specific arrangement of these universals that will yield a further structured universal, namely methane. By Armstrong's own criteria for the existence of universals, it looks as though such structural universals should be allowed. For example, they seem to ground distinct causal powers: methane has causal powers distinct from those of hydrogen and carbon, just as we noted that water has causal powers distinct from those of hydrogen and oxygen. Moreover, structural universals seem to be able to ground genuine similarities: two molecules of methane are genuinely similar, as they have the very same structural arrangements of the more basic universals.

In addition, as both Armstrong and Lewis note, structural universals may need to be at least possible on Armstrong's account; for we cannot rule out the possibility that there may be no basic or fundamental universals. For instance, there may not be a fundamental level of being at which we can identify the basic universals, in which case, if there were to be any universals, they would *all* be structural. In the absence of being able to rule out such a possibility, we are provided with an additional reason to posit structural universals on Armstrong's account. This is an issue we will consider further in Chapter 6.

However, as we will see later in the book, allowing for structural universals does not go the full way to allaying our concerns about the ability of Armstrong's universals to meet the requirements set out by the one over many argument. This is because, even if we can make sense of structural universals such as being methane or being water, which are composed by a clear and uniform structure of simpler universals, not all of the examples of properties that we have been working with have this structure.

Take the property of being red, for example. Armstrong himself (1978b: Ch. 22) *denies* that redness is a universal, on the grounds that it is not something that can be understood in such a way. In fact redness seems to be a property that would be understood *disjunctively*, if it were to be understood structurally at all. This is because redness is a *determinable* property with many *determinates* – such as crimson, scarlet and vermillion, to take some examples.[15] These are all determinates of red because any object that is red will necessarily be one of these shades of red. But, of course, not all red objects will exhibit the same determinate: some will be crimson, some scarlet, some vermillion, and so forth. But now notice that this makes redness itself more of a disjunctive property than a structural universal. This is because every red object will exhibit one of the shades of red: it will either be crimson or scarlet or vermillion – and so on. But, if this is the case, then redness seems to fail the genuine similarity constraint; for not all red objects will exhibit the kind of identity required for the sharing of a universal: a crimson car and a scarlet scarf, for example, are not identical with respect to their redness. Here is how Armstrong puts it:

> Suppose that *redness* is a property which all red particulars, whatever their shade of red, have in common. Since properties are universals, this entails that the particulars are *identical* in a certain respect: in respect of their redness. Now consider particulars of a different shade of red. It is in this very respect of *redness* that they differ. Yet it is impossible that things be identical and different in the very same respect. It is undeniable that different shades of red are different properties. If

follows that *redness* is not a property common to all red things. (Armstrong 1978b: 117)

This argument is quite general and applies to all our general colour predicates – and also to the predicate 'is coloured' itself. If properties are identified with universals, then there are very strict requirements on what it takes to be a property: the particulars that instantiate it must be identical in that very respect in order for the thing in question to be considered a property. Being similar in certain respects is not enough; for that will not secure identity. As a result, despite the allowance of structural universals, there will be many things we intuitively think of as properties that will turn out not to be properties on Armstrong's view.

In later work (1997b: Chs. 3 and 4), Armstrong offers a more sophisticated account of determinates and determinables, which seems to lean more towards the pluralist proposals we will examine in Chapter 6. With regard to determinates (such as scarlet, crimson and vermillion in our example), he suggests that these may be considered universals that are related through *partial* identity. Armstrong (1997b: 51) gives two cases of partial identity, which can both be illustrated by conjunctive universals, which we discussed earlier. The first kind of partial identity is that which holds between a part and a whole, for example between the simple universal P and the conjunctive universal P&Q. Here it can be said that P&Q is partially identical to P, as it contains P as a part. The second kind involves overlap, such as in the case where we have two conjunctive universals, P&Q and Q&R. P&Q can be said to be partially identical to Q&R, as they both share something – Q; but they are not wholly identical, as they each have different parts in addition to Q.

It is not clear whether this helps in all cases of determinates, however. Consider the colour case again, and suppose that we are looking at the part of the colour spectrum that includes all the determinates of red. We can imagine these plotted along a line, so that, for example, scarlet occupies the point that reflects light between wavelengths a and b, crimson occupies the point that reflects light between wavelengths c and d, and vermillion occupies the point that reflects light between wavelengths e and f. We can note that each determinate *must* occupy a distinct point on the spectrum; and there cannot be overlap between determinates, because it is a feature of determinates that they necessarily exclude one another – nothing can be both scarlet and crimson at the same time, for example. The worry now is that neither of the accounts of partial identity seems to capture the relations between the determinates. The parthood account does not seem relevant here, as the determinates are not parts of each other; and the overlap account does not seem relevant either, as there are no points of overlap between one determinate and another – they each occupy distinctly demarcated points on the colour spectrum. So it is unclear whether the move to partial identity would do much to unify the things that have different determinates.

Moreover, even if a successful story could be told here, this would not mean that *determinable* properties such as redness come out as universals on this amendment. On the contrary, Armstrong still denies that they are universals, but he weakens his position somewhat to allow that they be what he calls '"second-class" properties' (1997b: 43–6). They are taken to be 'second-class' because they depend on the universals (the 'first-class' properties) for their existence and instantiation. While this is a step in the direction of the pluralist proposals we will consider in Chapter 6, it is not clear at this stage what kinds of things we should take such second-class properties to be. Consequently we will defer further discussion of this idea until Chapter 6, where we will have more concrete proposals to consider.

2.3.5 Armstrong on Reference and Quantification

So far we have focused on the *metaphysical* features of properties that we identified in Chapter 1, and it is clear that Armstrong intends to take those very seriously indeed. But what is his view about the *semantic* features that we identified – namely the need for properties to serve as referents for our predicates, or to be things that are quantified over in ordinary sentences?

Bearing in mind what we have seen in relation to Armstrong's Eleatic and exclusion principles, it is clear that he does not put much stock in semantic features. Indeed his forceful adherence to a posteriori method and his reliance on it for determining what universals there are suggest that it is the sciences, not any ordinary way of speaking, that should be of relevance here. Armstrong thinks that, if we are to make progress in matters metaphysical, we should not assume that our ordinary ways of speaking are accurate. Thus he does *not* think that we need properties to make sense of the meanings of ordinary predicates, and, especially when it comes to universals, he denies that there is a universal to serve as the referent for every meaningful predicate. This is primarily due to Armstrong's methodology: because he thinks that it is science, and particularly *physical* science, that tells us what ultimately exists, and because ordinary language cannot serve as a reliable guide to the findings of physical science, we cannot draw ontological conclusions from the meanings of terms in ordinary language. Thus the fact that we use the predicate 'is red' in ordinary language does not, according to Armstrong, justify us to posit a corresponding universal of *redness*: we would only be justified if this entity were to be posited by physical science.

We can also note, as Lewis (1983) points out, that Armstrong's universals are poorly suited to be the sort of things that are quantified over in the statements we examined in Chapter 1:

(5) He has the same virtues as his father.
(6) The dresses were of the same colour.
(7) There are undiscovered fundamental physical properties.
(8) Acquired characteristics are never inherited.
(9) Some zoological species are cross-fertile.

Of all of these, as Lewis notes, only (7) seems to be a statement that could be thought to quantify over universals. The other ones could not be thought of in this way, as virtues, colours, acquired characteristics and species are not suitable candidates for universals on Armstrong's account. This would also apply in the case of reference. Even though Armstrong himself does not take the reference argument seriously, we can note that, for the same reasons, universals cannot serve as the referents of predicates in our examples:

(1)   Red resembles orange more than it resembles blue.
(2)   Red is a colour.
(3)   Humility is a virtue.
(4)   Redness is a sign of ripeness.

As a result, Armstrong's universals are not the sorts of things that would satisfy the semantic reasons for positing properties that we identified in Chapter 1, and he does not consider the task of accounting for predicate reference to be of significance when giving a theory of properties:

> *The study of the semantics of predicates must be distinguished from the theory of universals.* Ontology and semantics must be separated – to their mutual benefit. (Armstrong 1978b: 12)

Despite these claims, we will see that Armstrong ultimately puts some stock in the semantic arguments for positing properties, particularly in his debate with the extreme form of nominalism. We will consider this issue further in Chapters 4 and 6.

2.3.6   Summary

We have now reviewed the main aspects of Armstrong's immanent theory of universals. As should be clear, there are a number of concerns, but, as we will see throughout the book, no theory is perfect. Armstrong's view remains one of the most influential theories of properties around, and we will continue to evaluate it in relation to other views as we continue through the book.

Before we move on, it is worth making one final point about the connections between the two main aspects of Armstrong's view, namely the immanent universals proposal and the a posteriori methodology. Some of the main problems we have identified for immanent universals seem to stem from Armstrong's methodological background, which defers to natural science when it comes to determining what universals there are. One might wonder whether there are different ways to take the general proposal of universals as immanent – ways that do not take such a methodology on board, and thus avoid some of the central problems discussed. This is certainly a possibility to explore; but it is worth sounding one cautionary note. On the immanent universals proposal, every property is an immanent universal, and in consequence every property that an object has must be a part of that object. If we take this on board but want to lift the restrictions on the sorts of things that count as immanent universals, then we might run into some strange results. For instance, to take an example from David Lewis (1986b: 67), we might think that a particular bed has the property of having been slept in by George Washington. On the more liberal immanent universals proposal, though, to account for this property, we would need to say that the property of being slept in by George Washington is part of the bed, which – according to Lewis – is absurd! The lesson to draw is that any view that holds that properties are immanent universals but that wishes to reject Armstrong's general methodology may well still find itself just as restricted by the nature of immanent universals themselves.

2.4 Further Reading

For properties as transcendental universals, Plato's theory of the Forms is one of the most famous theories in philosophy. It is discussed in the middle dialogues and especially in Book 7 of *The Republic*; but it is perhaps given its most extensive and lucid treatment in the later *Parmenides*, where Plato himself subjects it to severe criticism coming from the character Parmenides. In the twentieth century the most prominent expression of this theory was given by Bertrand Russell in his *The Problems of Philosophy* (Russell 1967), Chapters 9 and 10. Sympathetic contemporary discussions include Macdonald 2005, Chapter 6, Bealer 1998, van Inwagen 2011, and Jubien 1997, Chapter 4, and 2009. At the time of writing, 'locationist' proposals of properties, which are also versions of the transcendental view, were start-ing to gather interest; such proposals can be found in the work of Stalnaker (1979) and Cowling (forthcoming).

To get the full story on Armstrong's universals, one should look at his 1978a and 1978b. Shorter and more recent state-ments of Armstrong's position can be found in his 1989, 1997a and 1997b. There is an extensive debate on the viabil-ity of structural universals, and a good place to start is Lewis 1986a. Armstrong 1986 offers a response to Lewis, and the discussion has continued in more recent times with Schaffer 2004, Williams 2007b and Hawley 2010. The issue of the viability of conjunctive universals in particular is debated by Mellor (1992) and Oliver (1992).

For those wanting to look beyond these views about uni-versals, there are alternative frameworks available. Two influ-ential examples are L. A. Paul's view of properties as 'logical parts', and E. J. Lowe's view which uses modes to understand properties in his 'four-category ontology'. For more on these views, see Paul 2002, 2006, and Lowe 2002, 2006.

3
Tropes

3.1 Introduction

In the last chapter we looked at the view that properties are universals, which took it that there was a fundamental distinction between two different kinds of entity: particulars and universals. The view that we will examine in this chapter is, perhaps, historically, the classic opponent of the universals theory, and it questions its basic claim that there is such a distinction at all. According to *trope* theory (our subject in this chapter), only *particulars* exist, and not universals. This is not to say, though, that trope theory is in the business of debunking properties, like the view that we'll encounter in the next chapter. Trope theory still aims to give an account of what properties are; and, on this view, what properties are is explained in terms of a special kind of particular: *tropes.*

We will begin by giving a brief statement of the theory before looking at some arguments for it – including the idea that tropes are well placed to account for the causal powers of objects. We will then turn to examine this view of properties in more depth, and we will discuss some problems it has in accounting for (1) the distinction between tropes and objects; (2) the relation between tropes and objects; and (3) the resemblance between tropes. The lesson to be drawn will be similar to that drawn in the last chapter: that it is not possible to explain everything without taking some things as primitives. At the end of the chapter we will note some similarities and differences between tropes and universals.

3.2   The Basic Idea

The starting point for the present theory is this. In the last chapter we saw that those who hold that universals exist do so in part on the grounds that there is some single thing that all the objects of a certain kind have in common. For instance, we observe that a range of different objects are metallic, and we conclude that there is something – metallicness – they all have in common. Metallicness is then accounted for in terms of a universal, metallicness, which is present in all of these instances. The trope theorist denies this final step in the reasoning. She notes that all we have observed is a bunch of *particular instances* of metallicness – the metallicness of a car, the metallicness of a fork, the metallicness of a wire – and she denies that these observations license one to infer that there is some single thing that exists in each of these instances. Rather what we have is a bunch of different instances in which metallicness in one is exactly similar to metallicness in the others.

The central claim, then, is that the car, the fork and the wire do not *share* something – metallicness; rather they each have their own particular instance of metallicness – in other words, each has its own metallicness trope, and this trope is entirely distinct to each. The initial grounding for a distinction between *object* and *property* is as follows. An object – as we will see – is generally taken to be a bundle of tropes, and the properties that an object has will be the tropes that make up the bundle. This will need some qualification, though. Strictly speaking, trope theorists say that a trope is a *property instance*, as opposed to a property full stop. That is, the metallicness of the fork is an instance of the property metallicness; and the property metallicness itself is taken to be the set of all the property instances of metallicness. So objects, strictly speaking, possess property instances, which are

V Imp

members of the set that constitutes the property in general. We will return to this idea and its justification shortly.

Before we move on we should make one terminological point. The term 'trope' is one term among many for the kind of entity under discussion here. For example, some trope theorists, such as D. C. Williams and Keith Campbell, prefer to use the phrase 'abstract particulars' for tropes, in contrast to whole objects, which they refer to as 'concrete particulars'. The general thought behind this distinction is that the metal-licness of the wire, for example, is a part of the wire and is considered so because it is a feature of the wire that we can 'abstract' from the wire as a whole: we can think of metal-licness independently from any other features of the wire. As Campbell himself puts it:

v. Imp

> In this context, an item is abstract if it is got before the mind by an act of abstraction, that is, by concentrating attention on some, but not all, of what is presented. A complete mat-erial body, a shoe, a ship, or lump of sealing wax, is concrete; all of what is where the shoe is belongs to the shoe – its color, texture, chemical composition, temperature, elasticity, and so on are all aspects or elements included in the being of the shoe. But these features or characteristics considered individu-ally, e.g., the shoe's color or texture, are by comparison abstract. (Campbell 1997: 126)

A feature of the shoe is thus considered abstract when it is considered alone, in separation from any other features of the shoe. But the shoe itself – considered as a whole – is taken to be concrete. However, in what follows we will not adopt the phrases 'abstract particulars' and 'concrete particulars', primarily because using these designations complicates trope theory rather needlessly. Firstly, as Daly (1997: 142–4) points out, there is no clear way of grounding their distinctions between concrete and abstract particulars, which complicates the relations between tropes and objects. Secondly, as Simons (1994: 557) notes, the uses of the terms 'concrete' and 'abstract' here are rather idiosyncratic and, confusingly, do not match up with the more general philosophical uses of the terms that we discussed in Chapter 2. As the complications introduced by using the phrases 'abstract particulars' and 'concrete particulars' do not affect trope theory in general, we will put them aside whenever possible for the rest of this discussion.

3.3   Tropes and Causation

We noted in Chapter 1 that one of the features properties are taken to have is to ground the causal powers of objects, or to feature in analyses of causation. Trope theorists argue that tropes can be used to account for this feature. Consider the following example, which comes from Campbell:

> The weakness of the cable caused the bridge to collapse. (Campbell 1997: 129)

If we subscribe to a theory of universals such as those examined in the last chapter, it looks as though we would have two candidates for the cause of the bridge's collapse: the particular – the cable; and the universal – weakness. However, argues Campbell, neither of these seems correct, as the universal is far too general in this case, whereas taking the particular as a whole introduces a whole host of features that are not pertinent to the event:

> It is the weakness of this particular cable, not weakness in general or the weakness of anything else, which is involved in the collapse of this bridge on this occasion. And it is not the cable's steeliness, rustiness, mass, magnetism, or temperature, which is at all involved. To hold that the whole cable, as concrete particular, is the cause of the collapse is to introduce a mass of irrelevant characteristics. (Campbell 1997: 129)

However, Campbell claims, tropes are far better placed to account for the cause of the collapse of the bridge:

> The cause of the collapse is the weakness of this cable (and not any other), the whole weakness, and nothing but the weakness. It is a particular, a specific condition at a place and time: so it is an abstract particular. It is, in short, a trope. (Campbell 1997: 129)

Campbell's claim is that, in particular instances of cause and effect, tropes are very well placed to account for the causation involved, as it tends to be the particular occurrence of some particular feature that causes a particular effect. He thinks that, if we use universals to try to explain causation, we have to hold that the universal itself is involved in the causal process; but recall that the universal itself is – on Armstrong's view at least – multiply located, so each instance of the universal in all of its locations would be invoked to explain just one particular event.

What about more general causal claims, though, such as the claim that things that have the property of being metallic conduct electricity? Law-like statements like this seem to pose less of a problem for the theory of universals, as they really do seem to make reference to each instance of a universal: the claim above is essentially a claim to the effect that metallicness – wherever it is found – has the propensity to conduct electricity. Thus Campbell's complaint about involving universals in causation – which is made on the grounds that universals would bring in concerns that are too general – does not seem to apply. One question to ask here is whether the trope theorist faces almost the reverse objection – stemming from a problem opposite to the one she raises for the universals theorist: are tropes too particularised to be able to make sense of general law-like statements?

The answer to this question triggers some of the apparatus that we briefly mentioned earlier, which involves the notion that tropes form sets. The idea is that, when we have, say, two or more tropes of metallicness, the trope theorist holds that these tropes are exactly similar. How she accounts for exact similarity is something we will discuss later, but the rough idea is that exactly similar tropes will form a set: in this case, the set of metallic tropes. So the metallicness of a car, the metallicness of a fork, and the metallicness of a wire will all be members of the set of metallicness tropes. The set of metallicness tropes will contain each particular instance of metallicness. With this idea up and running, the trope theorist is able to provide an account of law-like statements such as 'things that have the property of being metallic conduct electricity'. The claim here is that 'being metallic' refers to the *set* of metallicness tropes; in effect the claim is that each member of that set – each metallicness trope – has the propensity to conduct electricity. In this way the trope theorist is able to account for general statements of cause and effect.

3.4 Properties as Sets of Tropes

This discussion leads us nicely to the idea that tropes form sets and to the idea that properties are to be identified not with individual tropes, but rather with sets of tropes. We have noted one reason why sets might be needed – namely in order to deal with general causal statements; but, if we return to our original reasons for positing properties in Chapter 1, will find a more direct route. Recall the reference argument, which sought to find meanings for general property terms in statements such as 'red is more similar to orange than blue'. These seem to be general statements about properties and the relations between them; but they don't seem to be statements about any *particular* instances of these properties. Note the difference between the example given above and a statement like 'the redness of this rose is more similar to the orangeness of this orange than it is to the blueness of the sky'. This second statement refers explicitly to particular property instances, so we can easily use tropes as the referents of the terms in question; but this is not the case with the first statement.

The solution, as before, would be to hold that the term 'red' refers not to any particular redness trope, but rather to the *set* of redness tropes; and likewise 'orange' and 'blue' would refer to the set of orangeness tropes and the set of blue tropes, respectively. So, on this view, when we talk about the property of *being red*, we do not talk about any *particular* redness trope; rather we talk about the *set* of redness tropes. As a result, even though tropes play an important role in how we understand properties, properties themselves are not in general identified with tropes; rather they are identified with sets of tropes. However, it is important to note that *particular instances* of properties, such as the redness of *this* rose, *are* identified with tropes, the idea being that the general property of being red, for example, is the set of the particular instances of redness. This has the consequence that some of the jobs of properties, such as the grounding of particular causal powers, are discharged by property instances (tropes), while others, such as the grounding of more general causal powers, are discharged by sets of tropes (properties). It is also important to note that this account of the semantic values of predicates comes with a proviso: many accounts of tropes share Armstrong's view that it is not the case that every predicate refers to a property. (More on this later.)

3.5   The Relation between Objects and Tropes

According to the view that properties are universals, there are two fundamental categories of being, particulars and universals, bound together – whether tied by a primitive relation of instantiation or fused in a state of affairs. The forms of trope theory we have examined so far reject the view that there are two fundamental categories; and they do so in favour of postulating just one: particulars.[1] But trope theory does want to preserve the idea that whole objects are distinct from their properties. How exactly does this work, and what is the relation between objects and properties on this view?

The particular question of interest here is how tropes come together to form an object. There are two initial strategies that we will examine, namely the substratum option and the bundle theory. According to the substratum option, what binds tropes together is the fact that they are all possessed by a *substratum*. On this view, an object consists of a substratum that instantiates all the relevant tropes, plus the tropes themselves. Thus, for example, a table consists of a substratum plus the tropes of woodenness, solidity, brownness, and so forth. The substratum is both the thing that possesses the tropes in question and the thing that binds all the tropes together (they are all possessed or had by the same thing). We can note that positing the existence of substrata does not violate the idea behind the view that only particular things exist, as these substrata are also taken to be particulars.

Indeed they are often referred to as *bare particulars* – because, being the kinds of things that are supposed to possess tropes and to bind them together, they must be capable of existing independently of any of these tropes. In other words, they should not be thought of as having tropes of their own, hence their 'bareness'. As C. B. Martin puts it:

> If properties are not to be thought of as parts of an object, and the object is not then to be thought of as a collection of properties, as its parts may be, then there must be something *about* the object that is the bearer of properties that under any description need to be borne. And *that* about the object is the substratum. (Martin 1980: 7–8)

The bare particular is thus 'bare' because it must be capable of existing independently of any of the tropes it possesses in order to be the sort of thing that both possesses the tropes and binds them together.

We saw in Chapter 2 that Armstrong rejects the existence of bare particulars, and indeed there are good reasons for doing so. Daly (1997), for example, notes some central problems. The first, due to Campbell, suggests that bare particulars are not, in principle, distinguishable from one another on the grounds that, by definition, they do not have any properties:

> The problem with bare particulars is that they have no properties. But if they have no properties they must be absolutely indistinguishable from one another. So how is it possible for there to be more than one of them? (Campbell 1990: 7)

In other words, for bare particulars to be the basis for all the various objects we encounter, there must be a plurality of them. But, Campbell asks, how is this possible, given that, in principle, they are indistinguishable from each other due to their complete lack of properties?

So there are difficulties with the coherence of the very notion of a substance that exists in separation from any properties – in a state of lack of properties, as it were.[2] More-over, and perhaps more pertinently to this particular issue, it is not clear that this account would offer much beyond what the theories of universals that we encountered in Chapter 2 offered. For one thing, if we admit these two different kinds of particular, we need to show how they are related. In particular, we would need to show how the bare particular *instantiates* its tropes. But, as we saw in the last chapter, it is not possible to give an informative analysis of instantiation on pain of regress, and this applies here too, since instantiation, being a relation, would need to be explained in terms of tropes. In other words, positing bare particulars to explain how tropes are brought together offers us no progress in the absence of a satisfactory account of how the bare particular and its tropes are related.

The substratum option thus faces some significant problems. However, we can note that most of those who favour tropes prefer instead a 'bundle' account of particulars. On the view outlined by Campbell and Williams, for example, objects are thought of as bundles of tropes. That is, tropes are 'the very alphabet of being', as Williams puts it (Williams 1997: 115). On this view there is but one fundamental category, which is the category of tropes. Objects are derivative entities; they depend on tropes for their existence. This idea takes objects to be *bundles* of tropes, so the shoe that we discussed earlier will be constituted by a bundle of countless different tropes: a brownness trope, a solidity trope, a leather trope, and so on. On this view there is no underlying substance that possesses the tropes; the tropes themselves constitute the entirety of the object.

Objects are, then, bundles, or clusters, of tropes – and nothing more. You and I and the objects of our acquaintance are, on this view, different bundles of tropes. Of course, each bundle will be distinct, as each trope is a particular, so even two very similar objects will be different bundles by virtue of being constituted of different tropes. We cannot stop the story here, though, as we need to say something about how tropes form bundles; how they are clustered together to form an object.

The standard method here is to use a relation of *compresence*. That is, we consider objects to be bundles of compresent tropes: tropes that are bound together by their occupying the same point in space and time.[3] The thought is that what binds tropes together is their being located at the same place, and sharing this location is the relation that is given expression to by *compresence*. So, the thought is, an object is a bundle of tropes that are all located at a particular point in space–time. However, problems arise for bundle theory as soon as we start to think more about this relation of compresence. Anna Maurin (2010) suggests that there are two ways to take this relation: internally or externally. She puts the distinction as follows:

> To say [of a relation] that it is internal, is to say of the relation that it depends for its existence on the existence of its relata and of the relata that they depend for their (joint) existence on the existence of the relation. To say of the dependence that it is external is to say just the opposite; the relation exists independently of the existence of its relata, and the relata exist independently of the existence of the relation. (Maurin 2010: 321–2)

An example of an internal relation would be the relation in the sentence '3 is greater than 2'. It is part of the nature of the numbers 3 and 2 that that they are related in such a way that 3 is greater than 2, and they would not be the things they are if they were not related in this way. An example of an external relation, on the other hand, would be the relation in the sentence 'Katherine Hepburn has won more Oscars than Elizabeth Taylor'. The relation 'has won more Oscars than' is external because it is not part of the essential nature of Katherine Hepburn that she has won more Oscars than Elizabeth Taylor, nor is it part of the essential nature of Elizabeth Taylor that she has won fewer Oscars than Katherine Hepburn: both could have existed with their essential natures intact if they were not related in this way. Returning to tropes and to compresence, if we take the compresence relation internally, then the fact that two tropes are compresent will be explained by some fact about the nature of those tropes themselves: that there is something about them that makes it the case that they *must* be compresent. If the relation is taken externally, however, there will be no such constraint, and we are free to understand it in terms that do not depend on the natures of the particular tropes themselves.

Let us first consider the internal interpretation. If the relation is internal, then two tropes must be compresent in virtue of their very natures: it must be part of the nature of one that it is compresent with the other. But this does not look right, for in many cases the tropes that come together in a bundle need not necessarily be compresent. For example, take a crimson key, which – we suppose – is a bundle of tropes, including a crimson trope and a metallic trope. On the internal account, the crimson trope and the metallic trope are related in such a way that it is part of the nature of one that it must be compresent with the other. But this cannot be correct; for the key could have been not crimson, or indeed it can change its colour, all the while remaining metallic. It thus looks as though internal relations are the wrong way to think about bundles, for they seem to make every property essential in the sense that the object would be unable to lose a property without losing all the others.

Let us now turn to the external understanding. Compresence is a relation, and if the compresence of two or more tropes is not to be understood with reference to the natures of those tropes, then we must understand it some other way. Given that compresence is a relation, if we are to stick to the terms of trope theory, we can note that it must itself be understood as a trope. But now problems start to arise in the form of two infinite regresses. As Ehring (2011: 120–1) notes, there are two regresses, and which one kicks in will depend upon whether one takes the relation of compresence to be itself a part of the bundle of tropes that it is relating. If one thinks that compresence should be included in the bundle, then the first regress results:

> *Regress argument 1*: we begin with two assumptions: (1) an object is a bundle b of mutually compresent tropes, and, for every pair of tropes, t_1 and t_2, in the same bundle b, there is a compresence trope, say c_1, linking those tropes; and (2) every compresence trope linking tropes in that bundle is also in that bundle. From (1) and (2), we can infer that c_1 is in bundle b and that there is a compresence trope, c_2, linking t_1 and c_1 (as well as linking t_2 and c_1). But then c_2 is also in the bundle and there must be a compresence trope linking c_2 to c_3, and so on. This is a vicious regress. (Ehring 2011: 120)

So, if compresence tropes are parts of the bundle itself, we will also need to explain what makes them part of the bundle.

According to the standard story, what makes a trope a part of a bundle is that it is compresent with the other tropes in that bundle. As compresence is a trope, a compresent trope will need to be compresent with other tropes in order to be part of the bundle. But then we will need a *further* compresence trope to account for this, and so on ad infinitum. This suggests that we cannot account for compresence in this way.

What about if we do not consider compresence tropes to be parts of the bundles they bind together, or at least we decide not to take a stance on the issue? Unfortunately this offers little promise, since, as Ehring notes, another regress awaits:

> *Regress argument 2:* for tropes t_1 and t_2 to be compresent, they must be linked by a compresence trope, say c_1. But the existence of tropes t_1, t_2, and c_1 is insufficient to make it the case that t_1 and t_2 are compresent since these tropes could each be parts of different, non-overlapping bundles. For t_1 and t_2 to be linked by compresence trope c_1, c_1 must be compresent with t_1 by way of a further compresence relation, say c_2 (and with t_2 by, say, c_3). However, the existence of t_1, c_1, and c_2 is insufficient to make it the case that t_1 and c_1 are compresent – since each of the latter could be parts of different bundles. For t_1 and c_1 to be compresent by way of compresence trope c_2, c_2 must be compresent with t_1 by way of a further compresence trope, say c_4, and so on. This is a vicious regress. (Ehring 2011: 121)[4]

In this case we do not say that compresence tropes need be parts of the bundles; but further problems arise. It is not enough just to say that tropes t_1 and t_2 exist, along with compresence trope c_1; for this does not rule out the possibility that they exist but are not related in the correct way (it is possible for t_1, t_2 and c_1 to exist without t_1 and t_2 being related by c_1). The mere existence of the compresence trope is not enough, so we need to posit a *further* compresence trope, c_2, to ensure that t_1, t_2 and c_1 are all compresent. But then the mere existence of this new compresence trope is not enough; is it is still possible that t_1, t_2, c_1 could all exist without being related by c_2. This would introduce the need for a further compresence trope, but it should be clear by now that this will just reintroduce the same problem; and we are stuck in an infinite regress.

In the face of such regresses, what might the trope theorist do? One obvious option is to take a lead from the responses to regresses that we noted in Chapter 2. This is to take compresence to be primitive and incapable of the kind of explanation standard relations are taken to have. This is effectively the same option that, as we saw, the theory of transcendental universals has to take on the matter of the relation between a particular and a universal; and Armstrong takes an equivalent position on the matter of the instantiation of immanent universals.[5] As we have seen and will continue to see, every view under consideration has to take something as primitive, so there is no shame in the general strategy. However, one potential cost for trope theory would be a *proliferation* of primitives, since – as we will see later – for more regress-related reasons, trope theory also has to take the resemblance between tropes to be primitive. If taking things as primitives is a vice in a theory, then one would want to minimise this vice as much as possible, especially if competitors are able to get by with fewer primitives.

Simons (1994) offers a different option, which he calls the 'nuclear' option. This view aims to blend some of the features of the substratum option and of the bundle theory so as to offer a more promising direction. Simons suggests that we consider two stages in the process. In the first stage, we have a collection of tropes that are a collection in virtue of the *internal* relations between them. These tropes form the essential properties of the object, and thus it is not a problem to use internal relations to relate them. These tropes constitute what Simons calls the 'essential kernel or *nucleus*' of the object (Simons 1994: 567). This is only the first step in the analysis, as many objects have more properties than just their essential ones. Simons's next move is to say that the non-essential properties that an object has may be considered to be borne by the nucleus: that is, the nucleus serves as the bearer of the non-essential tropes.

As a result, we have a view that Simons thinks improves on the other options. Unlike the pure bundle theory, we have something that possesses non-essential tropes; and, unlike the substratum option, we do not need to posit bare particulars in order to get this result but just internally related essential tropes. We also preserve the distinction between essential and non-essential properties, which is lost when we take *all* the relations to be internal – because only the essential tropes are internally related.

However, while it solves some of the problems that the substratum option and the two forms of the bundle theory faced, this proposal does not solve them all. A glaring problem is the relation between the nucleus and the tropes that are possessed by the nucleus. Here it seems that we are stuck with the same problems we encountered before. The relation cannot be internal, for these are not properties that the nucleus has essentially. But then, if we take it to be external, we get the same problems we had with compresence for the version of the bundle theory that took compresence to be an external relation. Indeed this is pretty much the very same problem that the substratum theory posed when we were trying to account for the instantiation of tropes through bare particulars. Once again, we are left with the familiar option of having to take *something* as a primitive, and here that something will be the relation between the nucleus and the peripheral tropes. So, while some problems are solved, particularly the problem of distinguishing between essential and non-essential properties, which the internal version of bundle theory suffered from, it is unclear how this represents a significant progress from the external version of bundle theory.

3.6 Accounting for Resemblance between Tropes

We have noted that resemblance between objects is understood in terms of those objects having exactly resembling tropes. Thus the resemblance between a rose and a London bus is that each has exactly resembling crimson tropes. These tropes are distinct and separate things; resemblance is not the same as them sharing a universal, since in that case they would have one and the same thing – a universal – in common. According to trope theory, though, they do not share one and the same thing in common, rather they instead have exactly resembling tropes. While this account answers one question of resemblance – the way in which distinct objects resemble one another – it leaves another question unanswered, namely how *the tropes themselves* resemble one another. On the account outlined above, the resemblance between two crimson objects is explained in terms of them having exactly resembling crimson tropes, but now we must ask: in virtue of what do the crimson tropes exactly resemble one another?

There is a very real concern that we will be launched on a regress similar in structure to the one we found in analysing resemblance for transcendental universals in Chapter 2.[6] The thought is that we understand resemblance between objects in terms of them having exactly resembling tropes. So, for example, the rose and the London bus will each have a trope that exactly resembles the other. Let us call them T1 and T2. But how do we now account for the resemblance between the crimson tropes T1 and T2? If we follow the account, it looks as though the resemblance between T1 and T2 must be explained in terms of *them* having exactly resembling tropes: that is, what makes the crimson tropes resemble each other is the fact that *they themselves* have exactly resembling tropes. Let us call these tropes that T1 and T2 have P1 and P2. But now we must ask: in virtue of what do P1 and P2 resemble each other? The answer, again, will be that P1 and P2 themselves have exactly resembling tropes – call them O1 and O2. But then, again, we must ask: in virtue of what do O1 and O2 resemble each other? And the answer will be, again, that they have exactly resembling tropes. This sequence will continue infinitely, constituting an infinite regress, and we will never be able to ground the resemblance between tropes. More seriously, if we are to understand the resemblance between objects in terms of resemblance between tropes and we cannot ground the resemblance of tropes, one might worry that, on this view, we cannot understand resemblance between objects after all.

One possible line for trope theory to take is to hold that exact resemblance between tropes is not to be understood in the same way as resemblance between objects. This is the direction taken by Campbell, who holds that we can think of exact resemblance between tropes as an *internal* relation of the same kind that we considered earlier with regard to compresence. On this account, two crimson tropes, for example, exactly resemble each other because of the very nature of those tropes. In other words, their very nature determines that they will exactly resemble each other. This seems more plausible in the case of tropes than it does in the case of objects, as, in most cases (those excluding essential properties), it does not look as though resemblance between objects is internal in this sense. For example, it is not part of the nature of a rose and a London bus that they resemble each other. It is somewhat different with the tropes themselves, though, for it does seem plausible to say that it is because of the very nature of the things they are that two crimson tropes exactly resemble each other.

Does this solve the problem, though? For it to do so it would need to block the move from two tropes exactly resembling each other to there being a relation of exact resemblance between them. If this move is made, then the latter must be a trope, and the regress above kicks back in. Campbell himself thinks that his account does block this inference, as he holds that one trope resembling another does not bring any substantial addition into being beyond the two tropes themselves:

> The only differences . . . between an exactly resembling pair of reds and an exactly resembling pair of greens is that the first pair are reds and the second greens. The *resemblings* do not have any added distinguishing character. (Campbell 1990: 72)

Campbell's move is thus to account for the exact resemblance between tropes entirely in terms of the natures of the tropes themselves, and to deny that this implies that there is any additional relation of resemblance between them. If there is no such relation, then there is no trope that causes the resemblance regress above.

Daly, however, questions the legitimacy of this move, doubting Campbell's ability to block the move from the exactly resembling tropes to there being a relation of resemblance between them. Here is his argument:

> it is true that, necessarily, if two concrete particulars have a red trope, then these particulars exactly resemble each other.

But it does not follow that there is no resemblance relation between them. Likewise, it is true that, necessarily, if an *exactly-resembles-with-respect-to-red* relation holds between two concrete particulars, then each of them is red. Yet it does not follow that they do not each have a red trope. But if the latter inference is rejected (as the trope theorist must reject it) then by parity of reasoning the former inference should also be rejected. (Daly 1997: 152)

If Daly wins this argument, then there is still an option available to the trope theorist. We have seen, and will continue to see in later chapters, that there is a strategy available in the face of such regresses, which is to give up trying to give a substantial explanation of the problematic notion in question and to take it to be primitive. Here the problem is the notion of resemblance between tropes, which, it seems, cannot be understood in terms of tropes alone, due to the infinite regress that arises. The move that the trope theorist can make is to say that, while resemblance between objects is to be understood in terms of tropes, resemblance between tropes themselves must be taken as primitive. This is much the same move we saw the two theories of universals we looked at in the last chapter make when it came to the instantiation of universals. There it looked as though there was no viable way of understanding instantiation, as any attempt to analyse it in terms of the theory of universals led to an infinite regress, so the only move available was the move to hold that the relation is primitive. This was accepted as an explanatory cost of the theory, but not as a fatal blow against it. Indeed, as we go through the book, we will see that none of the theories is able to escape taking some relation – and usually an important relation – as primitive.

3.7   Tropes and Universals

Trope theory has undergone something of a resurgence since Armstrong wrote *Universals and Scientific Realism* in 1978 (Armstrong 1978a). Indeed, part of its resurgence is due to the credence the view has been given by its opponents, such as Armstrong himself (see especially Armstrong 1989: Ch. 6).

As we will see in Chapter 6, David Lewis has also looked favourably on the view, even if he stopped short of endorsing it. With regard to the issue of whether universals or tropes should be preferred, it should be clear that there is no easy answer to this question. Neither view is perfect and both struggle with similar problems, such as over the relation between objects and properties. Neither view is completely hopeless either, though, and each has its own respective merits. Universals theory, for example, has a far simpler account of resemblance between universals than trope theory has of resemblance between tropes, whereas trope theory perhaps offers a more intuitive account of individual instances of causation. Moreover, both Campbell (1990: 45–51) and Lewis (1986b: 68/1997: 187) also argue that trope theory can account for structural tropes better than universals theory can account for structural universals. On the other hand, universals theory is able to make do with fewer primitives than trope theory, as universals theory only has one primitive notion (the instantiation of a property by an object), whereas the trope theories we have examined appear to have two (the relation of compresence between tropes and the relation of resemblance between tropes). As we saw in Chapter 2, theories that have fewer primitives have greater explanatory power than those with more, so – in the absence of any explanations for the trope theory's primitives – this will count as a point in favour of universals theory. Consequently, providing a better account of at least one of these relations is of paramount importance to trope theory in its comparison with universals theory.

One area where there does seem to be substantial agreement between the main versions of the theories is the issue of how many tropes or universals there are and what the relationship is between predicates and tropes or universals. Both Campbell and Simons share Armstrong's view that we should not draw ontological conclusions about what exists simply from the meanings of ordinary predicates. Thus Campbell:

> Trope theory is first and foremost a theory of the ontic constitution of the cosmos. It is a scheme to account for the patterns of variety, resemblance and order to be found there.

> That this world is a world of tropes is a thesis advanced quite independently of the existence of human thinkers that have developed language. (Campbell 1990: 24)

and

> There is, in short, no one-to-one correspondence between significant predicates and tropes. There can be fewer, or more, varieties of tropes than of predicates. Real patterns of resemblance, rather than the significance of discourse, call the tune. You cannot establish an expanded ontology just by constructing new meaningful predicates. (Campbell 1990: 25–6)

Simons takes the same view:

> It should be evident that I prefer what is known as a sparse theory of tropes, by analogy with Armstrong's sparse theory of universals: not just any old predicate we happen to use corresponds to a kind of trope. Which kinds of tropes there really are is in general a matter for empirical investigation rather than armchair pronouncement. (Simons 1994: 569)

With this in mind, we can note that at least some prominent versions of trope theory do not take the semantic motivations for positing properties seriously, privileging instead the metaphysical motivations. This is one point of similarity between the prominent forms of trope theory and the prominent form of the theory of immanent universals.

We can also note another point of similarity between the views – namely regarding the restrictions that are in place on the things that can count as tropes. According to trope theory, properties are identified with sets of tropes, and sets of tropes are identified by having exactly resembling tropes as their members. Thus, for two objects to share a property, they must each have a trope that exactly resembles the other. But now consider red, as we did in Chapter 2. There we saw that there does not turn out to be a universal of redness, as not all red objects are identical in respect of their redness: some are crimson, some scarlet, some vermillion, and so on. As universals were identified with properties, there was no property of redness on this account. We can note that the same conclusion is reached here; for not all red objects are exactly similar with respect to their redness – again, some are scarlet, some crimson, some vermillion, and so on. As a result, there will be no redness tropes, because it will not be the case that all red things exactly resemble one another with respect to their redness. If there are no redness tropes, then there is no set of redness tropes, and hence there is no property of redness.

Moreover, this will not just be the case with redness. Many of the things we ordinarily take as properties and use as ways to distinguish objects from one another will turn out not to be properties, because they will fail the exact resemblance test. This may not bother those who take the metaphysical reasons so seriously, but it does seem somewhat disingenuous in light of the reasons posited for thinking that there are properties in the first place. This is so *even* for the metaphysical reasons, where the one over many problem is often justified using examples of properties that do not turn out to be properties after all. Finally, as we will see in the next chapter, it is not so clear that those who adopt this sparse attitude towards properties are completely innocent of resting on the semantic reasons to some extent.

3.8   Further Reading

The classic statements of trope theory can be found in Stout 1921, 1923; Williams 1953, 1997; and Campbell 1990, 1997. Stout's view is also discussed in Landesman 1973. Simons 1994 is a significant work in the contemporary development of the view, and Maurin 2002, Ehring 2011 and McDaniel 2001 provide recent – although advanced – defences. Schaffer 2001 offers a discussion of the individuation of tropes. Daly 1997 provides a recent critical appraisal of the views presented by Williams and Campbell. Armstrong provides a critical, yet sympathetic, discussion of tropes in Armstrong 1989 (Ch. 6). For more discussion on potential responses to the regress problems for compresence, see Maurin 2010 and Ehring 2011 (pp. 121–35). An excellent resource for an extensive list of works on tropes is Maurin's entry on tropes in *Oxford Bibliographies* (Maurin 2013).

4

Properties Eliminated?

4.1   Introduction

In Chapters 2 and 3 we looked at views that attempted to
accommodate properties by positing special kinds of entities
(universals and tropes, respectively). In Chapter 5 we will
examine some nominalist views that aim to accommodate
properties without positing these special kinds of entities.
Before doing this, though, we will examine perhaps the most
extreme position in debates about properties, namely the
view that there is no need to accommodate properties at all
and that the reasons for positing such entities – which we
examined in Chapter 1 – are misguided.

   This extreme view is sometimes referred to as 'ostrich
nominalism' and is associated with Quine and his scepticism
about properties. Before addressing Quine's arguments
against properties, we will begin the chapter with a brief
introduction to his views on ontological commitment. We
will then explore his claim that sentences that seem to refer
to properties have paraphrases that do no such thing, and
that this frees us from any apparent need to commit to properties. We will note the significant problems that this approach
raises; and we will summarise the discussion between Devitt
and Armstrong on the matter. The chapter ends on the
thought that, while Armstrong can perhaps claim victory over
Quine and Devitt, his victory comes at the cost of demon-

strating that maybe he cannot distance himself from the semantic reasons for positing properties quite as much as he wants.

4.2 Russell and Quine on Ontological Commitment

We will start this chapter with a basic question: how do we decide which entities – and indeed which kinds of entities – are the ones to whose existence we are committed? Two of the key tasks of metaphysicians is to establish what there is and what that is like; but how do we set about giving answers to these questions? In other words, what *method* should we be using to decide what (sorts of) things exist?

One way to approach this question is to ask what has to exist in order for the sentences we utter to come out as true, or even as meaningful. A traditional view holds that, in order for our sentences to have meaning, the terms that compose them must refer. So, for example, for the sentence 'the rose is red' to be meaningful, the phrase 'the rose' must refer to an object and the phrase 'is red' must refer to a property. This of course entails that there *is* an object – the rose – and there *is* a property – redness – that the phrases in question refer to. The problem with this idea is that many meaningful sentences include terms that clearly do not refer to any objects: for example, 'Pegasus is a winged horse', or 'the present King of France is bald'. These sentences are meaningful, but it does not seem correct to say that they derive their meaning from existing entities to which (some of) their constituent terms refer.

In his famous article 'On Denoting', Bertrand Russell devised a strategy for dealing with these problematic cases, which he took to apply in general to sentences of the kind exemplified above (Russell 1905). Russell argued that, although sentences like 'the present King of France is bald' seem to have a standard subject–predicate structure, the correct logical form reveals otherwise. For Russell, sentences using definite descriptions, like '*the* present King of France', are actually disguised existential generalisations. What 'the present King of France is bald' actually says, according to

Russell, is that there exists some single entity that is the present King of France, and that this entity is bald. If you put it this way, there is no problem with attributing a truth value to the sentence: obviously there *does not* exist any such entity, hence the sentence is false.

Russell, and later Quine, also thought that this strategy would work with sentences involving proper names like 'Pegasus'. Russell argued for a 'descriptivist' account of proper names, which held that proper names should be understood as equivalent to definite descriptions. Thus 'Pegasus', for example, should be taken to be equivalent to a description – 'the winged horse of ancient mythology', for example. With this in mind, sentences like 'Pegasus flies' can be analysed in the same way as sentences explicitly involving definite descriptions: we simply substitute 'the winged horse of ancient mythology' for 'Pegasus' to get the sentence 'the winged horse of ancient mythology flies', and then we apply Russell's theory. This gives us the claim that there exists some single entity that is the winged horse of ancient mythology and that flies. Again, there is no problem with assigning a truth value, as the sentence is clearly false.

Russell's account was supposed to be perfectly general and not just to cover problematic sentences; and Quine noticed that it gives us a different way of looking at the kinds of entity our sentences commit us to. For instance, on the view that reference is paramount, the sentence 'the rose is red', if true, seems to commit us – as we saw – to the existence of an object – the rose – and a property – redness. But, if we use the Russellian framework, we find that things are not as they seem. On Russell's account, what this sentence says is that there exists some single entity that is the rose, and that it is red. Going beyond Russell, Quine pointed out that this does not seem to commit us to the existence of a property: all it commits us to is the existence of the rose to which, he suggests, the predicate 'is red' applies. We can paraphrase Michael Devitt (1980: 435/1997: 96) to specify this feature of Quine's view as follows:

(R)   The sentence 'the rose is red' is true iff there exists an object, x, such that 'the rose' designates x and the predicate 'is red' applies to x.

This can be stated more generally as:

> (G) The sentence 'a is F' is true iff there exists an object, *x*, such that 'a' designates *x* and 'is F' applies to *x*.

For the Quinean, there seems to be no reason for positing the existence of properties on the basis of the truth of sentences such as 'the rose is red'. This is because, for her, properties do not need to feature in the explanation of why a predicate applies to an object. Now this thought, of course, runs against one of the main reasons for positing the existence of properties that we noted in Chapter 1, and it has led Quine and others to suggest that the supposed 'one over many problem' is in fact a pseudo-problem.

4.3   Ostrich Nominalism

This attitude to properties has been referred to by Armstrong as 'ostrich nominalism', because he sees it as equivalent to putting one's head in the sand. For Armstrong, the Quinean is behaving like an ostrich when she advances analyses like (G) and refuses to accept that there is anything further to be explained. For Armstrong, (G) *does* leave something crying out for an explanation – namely this question: in virtue of *what* does the predicate 'is F' apply to *x* correctly? Armstrong, of course, will argue that a predicate applies to an object *because* the object possesses the relevant property: 'is red' applies to the rose *because* the rose *is* red (has the property of being red), and the Quinean's refusal to engage in the project of answering this question reproduces the behaviour of an ostrich.

Let us back up for a moment and consider the dialectic involved so far. Armstrong claims that the one over many problem consists in finding an explanation for sentences like the following:

> (1)   *a* and *b* have the same property, *F-ness*.

For Armstrong, the truth of sentences of this form requires the existence of properties, and this is one of the main reasons why he pursues his theory of universals. The Quinean is claiming that (1) can be paraphrased as follows:

(1p)   *a* and *b* are both *F*.

For Devitt, this paraphrase removes the overt commitment to properties, and he holds that (1p) is true just in case the following two claims are true:

(2)   *a* is F;
(3)   *b* is F.

Now, to establish the truth of (2) and (3), we apply the Quinean account and say, in the case of (2):

(G)   The sentence 'a is F' is true iff there exists an object, *x*, such that 'a' designates *x* and 'is F' applies to *x*,

and in the case of (3):

(G*)   The sentence 'b is F' is true iff there exists an object, *x*, such that 'b' designates *x* and 'is F' applies to *x*.

It is the truth of (2) and (3) that is needed to account for the truth of the initial sentence (1), Devitt argues, and, as we can see, the circumstances in which these claims are true do not require the existence of properties at all: they require just the existence of two objects to which the predicate 'is F' applies. Thus, for Devitt, the one over many problem is a pseudo-problem: citing sentences like (1) as evidence for the existence of properties is a mistake, as the truth of such sentences can easily be accounted for *without* requiring the existence of properties.

There are four main points at which Devitt's argument can be attacked. Firstly, as we have mentioned already, we can attack the claim that the truth of (2) and (3) does not require the existence of properties, on the grounds that properties are required to explain the application of predicates. Secondly, we can question Devitt's use of paraphrase in the move from (1) to (1p). In particular, we might wonder whether (1p) just makes implicit the ontological commitment made explicit in

(1), in which case – contrary to Devitt's claim – (1p) is still committed to the existence of properties, as are its components (2) and (3). Thirdly, we can question the Quinean account of the truth conditions of 'a is F' given in (G). Fourthly, even if one is sympathetic to Devitt's line, one might, as David Lewis (1983) has suggested, wonder whether Devitt has set himself too easy a task, in that his account does not seem to have the resources to deal with claims like:

(1L)   *a* and *b* share some common property,

where the shared property is left unspecified.

4.4   Primitive Predication

We have already discussed the first objection briefly: Armstrong argues that the Quinean's refusal to account for the application of predicates leaves him open to the charge of simply ignoring something that is crying out for an explanation. However, if we return to what Quine himself says, we find that, while Armstrong's frustration is not entirely unwarranted, his claim is not quite right either. Consider the following passage from 'On What There Is':

> One may admit that there are red houses, roses, and sunsets, but deny, except as a popular and misleading manner of speaking, that they have anything in common. The words 'houses', 'roses', and 'sunsets' are true of sundry individual entities which are houses and roses and sunsets, and the word 'red' or 'red object' is true of each sundry individual entities which are red houses, red roses, red sunsets; but there is not, in addition, any entity whatever, individual or otherwise, which is named by the word 'redness', nor, for that matter by the word 'househood', 'rosehood', 'sunsethood'. That the houses and roses and sunsets are all of them red may be taken as ultimate and irreducible . . . (Quine 1953: 10/1997: 81)

It is the last sentence here that should interest us at this point. Quine is not simply ignoring that predicate application seems to need explaining; he is claiming instead that *there is no explanation*, at least in the sense that Armstrong is after, that will account for predicate application in some other terms. Quine is claiming that the fact that 'is red' applies to houses, roses and sunsets is 'ultimate and irreducible' – does not admit of any *further* explanation – which is different from simply ignoring the issue, as Armstrong accuses him of doing (and compare Lewis 1983). The Quinean thus does *not* deserve the title of 'ostrich nominalist' because she does take a view on this issue rather than simply ignoring it.

The disagreement between Armstrong and Quine thus boils down to the following: the Quinean claims that the application of a predicate cannot, in principle, be explained – it is a 'primitive' fact – whereas Armstrong claims that it must admit of a significant explanation and, further, that such an explanation must involve properties. For the debate between them to proceed, *this* disagreement about the explanation of predicate application must be resolved. Later on in the chapter we will return to this issue and will discuss the possible implications that this dispute has for Armstrong's own view.

4.5 Paraphrase

The second way to object to Devitt's argument is to resist his use of paraphrase leading from (1) to (1p). Paraphrasing plays an important role in the Quinean account more generally, and our discussion of it here will take us further afield than Devitt's use in this instance. Devitt himself takes these issues to be separate from the one over many problem; but, given the important role that paraphrasing plays in his discussion of the argument, we need to address them here.

The Quinean's basic position is that paraphrasing can be used to remove apparent ontological commitments. Thus, according to her, while the existence of a property is seemingly required to make the following sentence true:

(a)   The rose has the property of being red,

it is not required to make true the sentence:

(a′)   The rose is red.

The Quinean proposes that (a') is a perfectly good paraphrase of (a), and thus equivalent to (a). As we have seen, according to the Quinean, all that (a') commits us to is the existence of the rose, not the existence of the property of being red. Hence, while the truth of (a) seemed to require the existence of a property, once we find the proper paraphrase of (a), we see that (a)'s being true did not make that requirement after all.

There are three main questions we can ask at this point. Firstly, is this an acceptable move? Secondly, if it is an acceptable move, does it work in every case? Thirdly, if it is an acceptable move and does not work in every case, does it work in Devitt's argument?

A famous negative answer to the first question was given by William Alston (1958). Alston argued that "good paraphrases carry their ontological commitments with them" (as Lynch 2009: 112 puts it), and thus one cannot use paraphrases to remove such commitments. Consider the matter in the following way. Take two sentences, S and S', where S' is a paraphrase of S. If S' is a good paraphrase of S, then it should be equivalent to S, in which case it is committed to the existence of the very same things as S. But if this is the case, then Quine's project is, at best, inconclusive: if (a') is a good paraphrase of (a), then all that this shows is that (a') is committed to the existence of the very same things as (a). But why suppose that Quine is right that (a') does not involve commitment to the existence of a property? In other words, why not suppose that (a) involves commitment to the existence of a property and that, as (a') is equivalent to (a), (a') also involves commitment to the existence of the property in question? The fact that (a') does not explicitly mention a property should not count as evidence, since (a') is, after all, equivalent to a sentence that does. In other words, if (a') is a good paraphrase of (a), then it ought to carry the very same ontological commitments as (a); but Quine has not yet given us reason to think that the commitments that are so carried do not involve commitments to properties.

The argument on the other side of the coin is, of course, to say that (a') *lacks* the ontological commitments that (a) has; but, according to Alston, if we say this, then we have to give up on the idea that (a') is a good paraphrase of (a). This is of no use to Quine, as he needs to show that (a) is not committed to the existence of properties *on the grounds that* it is equivalent to (a′), and if they are not equivalent then that project is scuppered.

If (a) and (a′) are good paraphrases of each other, then, if we take Alston's argument seriously, it is inconclusive whether they are committed to the existence of properties. Suppose, though, that the Quinean finds a way out of this impasse: what about the second question? Can paraphrases even be found in every case?

As Arthur Pap (1959) and Frank Jackson (1977) have pointed out, there is reason to doubt that they can find a way out, as a number of sentences that we would be happy to accept as true do not mention objects at all, just properties. Take, for example, the following claim:

(R)   Red is more similar to orange than blue.

(R) seems to just talk about properties and the relations between them, and it is clear that no immediately obvious paraphrase is available that would remove this feature. One suggestion, though, is to say the following:

(Rp)   Red objects are more similar to orange objects than blue objects.

This does not seem to work, though, since, while (R) seems true, (Rp) seems false. This is because there are many different respects in which objects can be similar to one another, and these often override colour similarities. For example, suppose you have a red table, a blue table and an orange elephant. If (Rp) were true, then the red table would be more similar to the orange elephant than to the blue table, which does not seem intuitively correct. Attempts to avoid quantification over properties by turning just to objects thus look difficult.

Things get even worse when we consider that there are some statements that *directly* quantify over properties, such as:

(C)   The dresses are both the same colour.

(C), if true, entails that there exists some colour which is possessed by both dresses. Without this colour being specified, it looks as though there is no way to paraphrase away the commitment to a property.[1]

To be fair to Quine, in later work he acknowledged the seriousness of these difficulties for the paraphrase project and accepted that sentences of this sort do give good reason to posit the existence of properties (Quine 1960). However, he stopped short of endorsing a view like Armstrong's and thought instead that we could make do with a form of *class nominalism*, which attempts to deal with properties through classes of objects. This is a view that we will explore in the next chapter.

So we have seen that the paraphrasing move is questionable and that, even if it does work in some cases, it cannot work in all. What about our third question: does it work for Devitt in his argument? It seems clear that, in its formulation at least, Devitt's paraphrase is not of the problematic form we just examined – although, as we will see in a moment, Lewis's 'harder' version of the problem is set up the problematic way. Whether Devitt's use in his version is appropriate will have to be settled by the viability of the approach in general. In the absence of any specific concerns with his particular paraphrase, the issue seems to come down to whether (1) makes explicit the commitments implicit in (1p), or whether (1p) shows us the true commitments of (1), shorn of any rhetorical flourish. At best, it looks as though this matter is at present undecided.

4.6 Objects and Properties

A third way to attack Devitt's argument is to question the semantic criterion laid down in (G). As Mellor and Oliver (1997: 15) have suggested, given (P) – which runs:

(P) 'a is F' is true if and only if there is a φ such that 'is F' designates φ and 'a' falls under φ,

and holds that *properties* are what is required to make the claims true – why think that (G), which takes *objects* to be central, is preferable to (P)? In other words, why suppose that (G), which takes *objects* to be the only things that need to exist, is preferable to (P), which takes *properties* to be the only things that need to exist? This point is strengthened when we consider some versions of the 'bundle' theory of objects, which hold that objects are nothing more than collections of properties.

If a successful case can be made for preferring (P) to (G), then Devitt's argument is cut off at a crucial stage and cannot be used to show that we do not need to posit the existence of properties. Devitt himself accepts the challenge raised by this point and does venture some arguments for (G) over (P). For instance, he claims that (G) is preferable because our 'best theories' commit us unequivocally to objects, but not necessarily to properties (Devitt 2010: 24). This is a contentious claim, however, and some have recently argued that our best scientific theories do not commit us to objects, the most prominent among these being perhaps Ladyman and Ross (with Spurrett and Collier) in their 2007 book *Every Thing Must Go*.

Devitt does point out that a victory of (P) over (G) would not entirely disrupt his aims, as it would still show that the one over many problem is not an important argument for postulating properties. This is because, if (P) is *already* the preferred semantic criterion, then we are committed to the existence of properties on the basis of that alone, and we do not need to use arguments from the one over many problem. If this were the case, then, although Armstrong would win the war, Devitt could still claim victory in the battle over the importance of the one over many problem.

4.7   A Revised One Over Many Problem

The fourth problem concerns the proper formulation of the one over many problem. As we saw, Devitt suggests that the problem is to explain the truth of sentences like (1):

(1)   *a* and *b* have the same property, *F-ness*,

when many such sentences are taken to be obviously true in everyday speech. However, David Lewis (1983: 355/1997: 201) suggests that (1) does not get to the root of the matter, as there are other sentences that require explanation, in particular those of the form:

(1L)   *a* and *b* have some common property (are somehow of the same type),

where the shared property is left unspecified. This raises a more serious problem for Devitt than (1) because he cannot paraphrase it into the claim that *a* and *b* are both *F*, as there is no mention of *F*. Also, he cannot paraphrase it by saying that there is some property, *F*, which *a* and *b* share, for to do so would be to quantify directly over the property. As was hinted at above, what we have is a difficult sentence of the form of sentence (C) previously discussed.

(1L) thus seems immune to Devitt's account of (1), so it seems that, phrased in this way, the one over many problem cannot be dismissed as a pseudo-problem in the same way as it previously was. Devitt (2010: 28) has noticed this, but still thinks that a paraphrase is available:

(1Lp)   *a* and *b* significantly resemble each other.

But notice now that we still cannot apply the same analysis for (1), and Devitt suggests that the Quinean takes (1Lp) to get to the root of (1L): all that (1L) says is that *a* and *b* significantly resemble one another, and there the explanation ends.

However, in doing this, Devitt shifts the Quinean from the position of an 'ostrich nominalist' about properties and suggests instead that two objects' sharing a property is explained in terms of their significantly resembling each other. As we shall see in Chapter 5, this is, in effect, a form of *resemblance nominalism*, which *does* attempt an account of what properties are. Lewis's amendment to the one over many problem thus seems to show that one cannot remain an ostrich; one must embrace a different form of nominalism.

4.8   Implications for Ostrich Nominalism

The original Quinean position was one that held that, at least when considering our ordinary speech, we are not committed to the existence of properties. The argument for this was – briefly – that any statement that seems to require the existence of a property in order to be true can be paraphrased by or recast into one that does not. Moreover, provided one is happy to accept primitive predication, this allows us to show that the standard one over many problem does not provide motivation for positing the existence of properties. We saw that Armstrong characterises this view as 'ostrich nominalism', but we also saw that this label is unfair, as the Quinean does not fail to recognise the call to explain predication – she just thinks that no explanation of the form Armstrong is after is available.

The question, then, becomes what kind of nominalism does the Quinean advocate: is it a distinct and extreme form of nominalism, or is it a view that ultimately collapses into one of the standard versions? We have seen that the view does seem to collapse, but it is open to debate which kind of nominalism it collapses into. Quine himself, for reasons related to the failure of paraphrasing across the board, seems happy to retreat to a version of *class nominalism*. Devitt, on the other hand, seems to advocate a retreat into *resemblance nominalism*. Which of these retreats is the most sensible one (and perhaps there are other options, too) will now most likely depend on which version of nominalism is the most plausible; and it is to that issue that we turn in the next chapter.

4.9   Implications for Universals and Tropes

Before we begin the next chapter, though, we should examine what has been said above in light of the theories of universals and tropes that we reviewed in the last two chapters. In particular, we should relate the discussion above to the claims that it is the metaphysical motivations for properties that we should take seriously, and not the semantic ones. We saw that both Armstrong and trope theorists dismissed in the strongest terms the idea that our ordinary predicates should serve as guides to what properties exist and the idea that many candidate properties that we ordinarily take to exist – such as redness – fail to exist as they fail to live up to the metaphysical requirements.

It is somewhat difficult to square this attitude with the line that Armstrong takes in response to Quine. For, in his argument with Devitt and Quine, Armstrong takes the application of a predicate to an object as a *key* thing to be explained by a theory of properties, and he admonishes Quine for – in his view – failing to offer an explanation. Likewise, Armstrong himself endorses the work of Pap and Jackson, to show that sentences such as 'red is more similar to orange than it is to blue' cannot be paraphrased away so as to become explainable in terms of just particular objects. However, both these moves look like odd moves for Armstrong to make, given the shape of his view as we saw it in Chapter 2: there explaining the application of predicates was not treated as a key job for properties to do, and there was an explicit denial of the existence of the properties (understood as universals) of redness (and, by the same token, also of orangeness and blueness, or so one assumes).

Perhaps, though, there is room for manoeuvre for Armstrong here. With regard to the first issue about predication, perhaps Armstrong can *agree* with Quine that – in most cases – the correct application of a predicate will *not* require the existence of a corresponding property. Indeed, that may well be the case with the predicate 'is red'. However, Armstrong will still deny Quine's claim that there is no explanation available, for in these cases there will be an alternative explanation for the correct application of the predicate – one that will not require a universal of redness.[2] The disagreement between him and Quine will kick in when we reach a predicate that *does* – for Armstrong – refer to a universal, for example 'is a quark'. Here Armstrong will insist that we *do* need a universal to explain the application of *this* predicate, whereas Quine will deny that such an explanation is needed. Armstrong can thus distinguish between the kinds of predicates that posit the existence of universals while still denying

Quine's claim that there is no analysis of predication; and he can do so by providing different analyses of different kinds of predications.

Things get a bit more tricky with his endorsement of Pap and Jackson's claims about the difficulty of paraphrasing. It looks as though an endorsement of their arguments would suggest an endorsement of the existence of the properties mentioned in the examples – namely redness, orangeness and blueness. But, if this is the case, then we seem to have inconsistency in Armstrong's claims that there are no such properties. However, Armstrong himself (1978a: 61) is careful to clarify what his endorsement of these arguments entails. For him, the arguments only serve to show that ostrich nominalism cannot account for the commitments of these sentences by using particulars alone. This does not mean, however, that we need to posit corresponding universals for the abstract singular terms in question; for, Armstrong thinks, there may be an alternative way of thinking about the issue, which would not require positing the universals of redness, orangeness and blueness. However, this will not be as simple as just positing the properties themselves, and, as Lewis (1983: 348–9/1997: 195) notes, it may well push Armstrong himself into having to adopt methods of paraphrase in order to account for the sentences, in the absence of straightforward reference to properties.

Be this as it may, it still points to an inconsistency in Armstrong's methodological approach. We saw in Chapter 2 that he does not think that ordinary language, and the use of ordinary predicates, should have *any* bearing on a theory of properties: this was part of his rejection of the semantic reasons for positing properties – which were also rejected by Campbell and Simons in the discussion of trope theory. Even though Armstrong may be able to square the analysis of predication and the unparaphrasable sentences with his theory of universals, the fact remains that he takes such things seriously *as things that are in need of explanation*. If he were to reject the semantic motivations fully, though, he would not even see the need to provide *any* explanation here. It is here, in this point, that the true inconsistency lies, when he uses these arguments against Quine and Devitt: these arguments require taking the semantic reasons for properties seriously, but that runs against his general methodological approach, which dismisses these reasons entirely.

Moreover, taking these reasons seriously throws Armstrong's theory – and trope theory – into new relief. When we evaluated the views before, the limitations on properties on these views were mitigated somewhat by the rejection of the semantic motivations. Indeed, it looked as though this feature was part of the general package: forget about the semantic reasons, and some (though not all) of the seemingly unpalatable consequences of taking properties to be so limited disappear. But, if these reasons are back in play, then the views are open to new dimensions of evaluation. In particular, as David Lewis (1983: 347–51/1997: 188–97) notes, we now have to consider the viability of the *semantic* picture that the views offer, as well as that of the metaphysical one. One obvious problem is that the views will have a far more complicated semantic account than views that are able to posit the existence of properties such as redness. In particular, when discussing sentences such as 'red resembles orange more than it resembles blue', Lewis says:

> *Prima facie*, these sentences contain names that cannot be taken to denote particular, individual things. What is the semantic role of these words? If we are to do compositional semantics in the way that is best developed, we need entities to assign as semantic values to these words, entities that will encode their semantic roles. Perhaps sometimes we might find paraphrases that will absolve us from the need to subject the original sentence to semantic analysis. That is the case with ['red resembles orange more than it resembles blue'], for instance. But even if such paraphrases exist – even if they *always* exist, which seems unlikely – they work piecemeal and frustrate any systematic approach to semantics. (Lewis 1983: 348–9/1997: 194–5)

Lewis's thought here is that, once we have the semantic reasons in play, we have to consider how our view of properties will fit with the best semantic theory. On his view, that theory would be one that assigns entities as the semantic values of predicates and abstract singular terms. But, of course, whatever moves Armstrong makes (or indeed the trope theorist) to accommodate the sentences in question without positing corresponding universals, that will be a more complicated theory, which will not fit as well with established semantic theory as a theory that *is* able to posit the existence of these properties up front.

The basic point to be made here is that, once the semantic motivations are accepted, semantic theory cannot be ignored, and a theory must also be judged on the semantic picture it gives. Lewis's point here is not that Armstrong – and the trope theorist – *cannot*[3] give an account of the sentences we considered, but just that theirs will be an account inferior to a simpler one, which allows for the properties that Armstrong – and the trope theorist – reject. This is an issue to which we will return in Chapters 6 and 7, but, for now, we can note that it strengthens the case for saying that Armstrong's theory and trope theory do not adequately accommodate the semantic features of properties.

4.10 Further Reading

As should be clear, the essential readings for this topic are the articles by Quine 1953, Devitt 1980 and 2010, Armstrong 1980 and 1997a, and Lewis 1983. In respect of issues with paraphrase, the articles by Pap 1959, Jackson 1977 and Alston 1958 are important. Also of interest are Armstrong 1978a: Ch. 6 and van Cleve 1994.

There has been extensive discussion of Quine's criterion of ontological commitment. Recent work by Rodriguez-Pereyra 2002, Heil 2003, Armstrong 2004 and Cameron 2008 has aimed to show that it is best understood in terms of truth-making, to which Schaffer 2008 offers a response. Other works of interest are Azzouni 1998 and 2010, Hodes 1990, van Inwagen 2004 and Schaffer 2009. Pickel and Mantegani 2012 argue that there is tension between Quine's criterion of ontological commitment and ostrich nominalism.

5
Varieties of Nominalism

5.1 Introduction

Suppose that we do not want to posit universals or tropes, but then we do not want to go with Quine either and deny the existence of properties altogether. There are quite a few options available at this juncture, most of which try to account for properties in terms of purportedly less controversial entities: predicates, concepts, classes and objects. In this chapter we will evaluate the viability of these options: predicate nominalism, concept nominalism, class nominalism, mereological nominalism and resemblance nominalism. These views are all varieties of 'nominalism', as they deny, or at least claim to deny, the existence of universals (though whether some of the views succeed in this matter is open to debate). They do not deny that properties exist though, and – for the most part – they readily give referents for predicate terms and entities to quantify over in statements such as 'she has the same virtues as her sister'. If the views succeed, they would thus have significant initial appeal: they would meet one of the main requirements for a theory of properties without positing mysterious universals or tropes. However, as we will see, things are not so simple, and, in the absence of universals or tropes, the views in this group seem required to take on questionable ontological commitments of different kinds. In other words, properties cannot be had for free, and whether the costs of doing without universals or tropes outweigh the benefits is an open issue in each case.

5.2 Predicate and Concept Nominalism

So far we have been taking broadly *metaphysical* questions as primary, asking what properties might be like and only afterwards thinking about how predicates might refer to them. However, a different approach to the subject is possible, which considers questions of *language* to be prior to questions of metaphysics. This approach addresses the issue of the nature of properties through the analysis of predicates; and the nature of properties will be explicable, in some sense, by reference to the predicates that express them. The basic idea, to use a popular expression, is that properties serve as the ontological 'shadows' of predicates. On this view, successful predication will automatically yield a corresponding property.

5.2.1 Pure Predicate Nominalism

Perhaps the most well-known formulation of pure predicate nominalism is that given in David Armstrong's (1978a: 11–24) discussion, despite the fact that Armstrong himself does not hold this view. Armstrong sets the view up as being committed to the following biconditional:

(P) An object, a, has a property, F, iff a falls under the predicate 'F'.

Taken as a global thesis, (P) holds that, for all properties, an object possesses a particular property, F, just in case that object falls under the corresponding predicate, 'F'. This thesis is taken to represent an *analysis* of properties, not an elimination – as is favoured by Quine, for example. The thesis holds that properties exist, and (P) is intended to lay down the conditions under which an object has a property.

After outlining this view, Armstrong raises two serious problems for it in the form of two vicious regresses, which he calls the *object* regress and the *relation* regress. Let us consider both in turn. Crucial to remember is that the view Armstrong is considering is the view that subscribes to (P), which holds that all properties (and relations) are to be accounted for by objects falling under predicates.

Let us take the object regress first. Armstrong supposes that predicate nominalism is attempting to give an account of unity to some extent. For example, all red things fall under the same predicate: 'is red'.

Now consider three predications: the rose is red; the fire engine is red; the car is red. Evidently, the predicate view will want to say that the three objects have the same property (redness), and the only way to do this is to say that they have the same property because they all fall under the predicate 'is red'. Notice, though, that the view is not immediately entitled to say this, as the three objects described all fall under different *tokens* of the predicate 'is red': one token is applied to the rose, another to the fire engine, and a third to the car. To get the idea that they share the same property, we have to say that they fall under tokens of the same *type*. So now we have to say that all of the 'is red' tokens are of the same type. But how do we get this? It seems that we have to say that all the red predicate tokens are of the same type because they all fall under the predicate 'is a "red" predicate'. But then, Armstrong suggests, we have to introduce a new type, 'being a red predicate', which now needs to be accounted for. What's the way to account for types? Falling under predicates; so tokens of red predicate predicates will fall under the predicate 'is a "red predicate" predicate'. This introduces a new type: 'being a "red predicate" predicate', which will again have to be accounted for in terms of predicates, and so on ad infinitum.

The second regress is a version of the familiar relation regress we have already encountered. Consider the relation of falling under – a relation that holds between an object and a predicate. The rose falls under the predicate 'is red'. Write the pair {the rose, 'is red'}, and we want to say that {the rose, 'is red'} instantiates the 'falling under' relation. How do we do this? We say that {the rose, 'is red'} falls under the predicate 'falls under'. But to do this we have to have a new pair: {{<u>the rose, 'is red'</u>}, <u>falls under</u>}, which instantiates the relation 'falls under' by falling under the predicate 'falls under'. But to say *this* we now need a new pair {{{<u>the rose, 'is red'</u>}, <u>falls under</u>}, <u>falls under</u>}, which instantiates the relation 'falls under' by falling under the predicate 'falls under'. But this will yield a *further* pair, {{{{<u>the rose, 'is red'</u>}, <u>falls under</u>}, <u>falls under</u>}, <u>falls under</u>}, which falls under the predicate 'falls under', and so on, ad infinitum.

Both regresses are taken to be vicious: the object regress shows that the predicate view cannot account for the crucial sameness of predicate type, and the relation regress shows that predicate nominalism cannot account for the crucial relation of falling under.

5.2.2   From Predicate Nominalism to Concept Nominalism

A different formulation is offered by Stephen Schiffer (2003) in what he calls his 'pleonastic' conception of properties. According to Schiffer, the existence of properties is 'secured' by what he calls 'something from nothing transformations'. He claims that, for subject–predicate sentences of the form 'a is F', we can immediately make a claim of the form 'a has the property of being F'. Thus, for example, from the sentence

(1)   'Poppy is a dog'

we can derive the sentence

(2)   'Poppy has the property of being a dog'.

This, according to Schiffer, is all there is to properties. We can say that properties exist, as their existence is immediately inferable from standard subject–predicate sentences, but they do not have any deeper nature than this. In other words, even in the case of the property of being a dog, there is no investigation into the nature of this property to be had: the nature of the property of being a dog is given entirely by the inference above.

Schiffer does not explicitly subscribe to Armstrong's (P) biconditional; and, if he can avoid subscription to it, this may allow him to avoid the vicious regresses. One method he might adopt is to say that all we need for (2) is the *truth* of (1). This does indeed seem to be required at some stage in the story, for it looks as though the inference:

(3) 'The moon is made of green cheese', so
(4) 'The moon has the property of being made of green cheese'

should not go through, on the grounds that (3) is false. In other words, *false* sentences should not be sufficient to *secure* the existence of a property. While it might be the case that (3) and (4) are *equivalent*, they are both *false*, so we should not make any positive ontological conclusions purely on the basis of (3), (4), or their relationship.

It is thus crucial that the starting subject–predicate sentence be *true* if we are to secure the existence of the property in question. That is, once (1), for example, is given the truth value 'true', we can immediately derive (2) from it. Is this all we would need in order to avoid the relation regress, though? A crucial matter, it seems, will be to establish that the truth of the starting sentence does not depend solely on the object in question falling under the predicate in question: that the truth of (1) in our example does not *depend* solely on Poppy's falling under the predicate 'is a dog'. Of course, Schiffer should not deny that Poppy falls under the predicate 'is a dog'; the real question is whether this is the *sole basis* upon which Poppy has the property of being a dog.

Unfortunately, Schiffer's own line seems to lead straight back into Armstrong's relation regress. Schiffer suggests that what establishes the truth of the starting sentences is the object's *falling under the concept* in question. He says:

> If something falls under the concept of doghood, we can't look at what it is apart from its falling under that concept, for there is nothing apart from its falling under that concept. There can be nothing more to the identity and individuation of a

particular property than is determined by the canonical concept for that property. This is why the property of being a dog has no hidden nature for empirical investigation to unearth; it is a shadow of the word 'dog'. (Schiffer 2003: 65–66)

For Schiffer, then, the truth of the starting sentences depends on the object falling under the concept in question. Given that the truth of the starting sentences secures the existence of the associated property, it follows that the existence of a property depends on the object in question falling under the concept in question. While this is not *exactly* the view specified by Armstrong, which declared that falling under a *predicate* was the key feature, it is a closely related view. In fact it turns out to be a view that Armstrong also considers (1978a: 25–7) and calls *concept nominalism*, which holds:

(C)   An object, a, has the property, F, if and only if a falls under the concept <F>.

If one were to combine this view with predicate nominalism and to hold that an object's falling under a predicate is determined by the concept associated with the predicate, then a route out of Armstrong's object regress presents itself. The puzzle there was to account for the sameness of the predicate type, which it seemed the predicate nominalist alone would be unable to do, as all he has recourse to in his theory is further predicates. However, by holding that the correct use of a predicate is determined by the concept associated with that predicate, the predicate/concept nominalist *can* account for the sameness of the predicate type: two token predicates are of the same type if and only if they are associated with the same concept.

However, as Armstrong notes, even if concept nominalism provides a route out of the object regress, the view is subject to the very same relation regress as predicate nominalism, as it has no additional resources to account for the relation of falling under, which holds between an object and a concept.

Both predicate and concept nominalism thus fall victim to Armstrong's relation regress. However, as we have seen before in the face of regresses, there is a potential way out. Indeed, both universals theory and trope theory are faced with regresses, in response to which they must take some things as primitives. In light of this, perhaps predicate and concept nominalists can avoid the relation regress by holding that the *falls under* relation is a primitive, and not an entity open to analysis. This may seem like a cop-out, but, as we have seen (and will see), most theories need to take some things as primitives. What the relation regress perhaps shows, then, is that predicate and concept nominalism need to take the relation of falling under to be primitive.[1]

5.2.3   Features of Predicate/Concept Nominalism

If this option is taken up, then we are free to assess the general features of predicate and concept nominalism to see if they are acceptable theories of properties; so, for the sake of interest, let us take up this option and hold the relation of falling under to be primitive. On this view we can state two (not necessarily entirely distinct) features of properties, as follows:

(1)   Properties are *abundant*: There are as many properties as there are predicates/concepts.
(2)   Properties are *secondary*: Whether an object possesses a property depends on whether the predicate/concept is correctly applied, not vice versa.

We can now consider some further objections to the view.

Regarding (1), there are two complaints that can be made. The first comes from those who think that this view makes properties too easy to come by. Properties, it is thought, ground important distinctions in nature; they divide objects into genuine kinds and 'carve nature at the joints'. However, many predicates/concepts do not have this function, and there are far more predicates/concepts than there are joints to be carved. If properties are just the shadows of predicates/concepts, then it looks as though they are unsuited to take on this crucial task.

The second complaint comes from those who think that the view does not admit enough properties: that properties are not abundant enough on this view. This complaint comes from David Lewis, who states:

> There are so many properties that those specifiable in English, or in the brain's language of synaptic interconnections and neural spikes, could be only an infinitesimal minority. (Lewis 1983: 346/1997: 192)

In other words, even those who are happy to be relaxed about the properties that exist would reject predicate/concept nominalism, because it does not go far enough: the number of properties is constrained by the number of predicates/concepts, but this is not acceptable if we have reason to think that there are far more properties than can be specified in language or thought.

Regarding (2), we can consider an example from David Armstrong (1997a: 161), in which a cold object becomes hot due to a heating process. Before the heating process, the object has the property of being cold, and after the heating process it has the property of being hot. According to predicate/concept nominalism, this is explained by the object falling under the predicate 'is cold'/concept <cold> before the heating process, and falling under the predicate 'is hot'/concept <hot> after the heating process. Armstrong is unhappy with this explanation though, holding that 'the change is something intrinsic to the object, and has nothing to do with the way the object stands to language' (Armstrong 1997a: 161).

Lying behind this claim is the thought that predicate/concept nominalism just gets things the wrong way around. Sentences are true *because* of ways the world is; the world is not a certain way *because* certain sentences are true. In particular cases, subject–predicate sentences are true when the object in question has the property referred to by the predicate: the sentence 'the object is hot' is true *because* the object is hot, whereas the object is not hot *because* the sentence 'the object is hot is true'; rather it is hot because of the movements of certain molecules. The charge is thus that predicate/concept nominalism drastically mischaracterises the relationship between language and the world.

We can now accuse predicate/concept nominalism of the mirror image of the problems we identified for universals and trope theory. That is, predicate/concept nominalism takes the semantic motivations for positing properties seriously, but does not adequately account for the metaphysical motivations. We noted that the reverse of this situation was bad for universals and trope theory, and we must now note that this situation is bad for predicate/concept nominalism.[2]

In addition to the problems discussed, the view that properties are the shadows of predicates (or concepts) provokes particular ontological puzzlement. This is because it holds that properties exist, but it has very little to say about exactly what they are. This is unlike other forms of 'nominalism', which offer *reductive* accounts of properties. For example, as we will see, class nominalism holds that properties are reducible to classes, and mereological nominalism holds that properties are reducible to (composite) objects. Predicate and concept nominalism stand apart, though, because they have no such account: they do not say that properties are *reducible* to predicates or concepts, holding instead that they are just *dependent* on them. The nature of these dependent entities remains a mystery, though. There is a number of options that the predicate or concept nominalist could take: she could hold that properties are abstract objects, the existence of which is secured by the kinds of procedures noted above. Alternatively, she could hold that they are sui generis entities that track the usage of predicates or concepts. One problem with these ideas, though, is that it gets increasingly unclear just how 'nominalist' these views are, even when 'nominalism' is understood only as the denial of universals or tropes. However the view turns out, though, there is still a difference between it and Armstrong's view of universals and trope theory, as the entities in question do not seem limited to the posits of empirical science, but the differences between them and the entities posited by the theory of *transcendental* universals are not clear.

Predicate and concept 'nominalism', then, if they are to be established as viable views at all, may not be forms of nominalism, given the nature of the entities they posit. What they seem to offer is sui generis entities – only they offer them in a more abundant number than standard views that adopt universals do. It is also worth noting that the question about the nature of these entities cannot simply be avoided by those who urge us to place questions of language prior to questions of ontology: even if the question of *whether* properties exist is trivialised, the question of *what they are like* still remains, and requires an answer. In the absence of any alternatives, it seems that even philosophers of this stripe are committed to the existence of (abundant) sui generis entities.

5.3   Class Nominalism

The idea that objects that share a property form a class might seem reasonably uncontroversial. Even those who think that properties are universals should perhaps be happy to say that the things that share a particular universal all form a particular class: the class of things that share that universal. Stepping back from universals for a moment, we can say, for example, that there is a class of human objects, all the members of that class being the objects that have the property of being human.

However, there is a controversial move that can be made if we take it that properties are *reducible* to classes. As Lewis puts it, 'to have a property is to be a member of the class' (Lewis 1983: 344/1997: 189). Thus, on this view, to have the property of being red is to be a member of the class of red things, and that is all. This view has the virtue of accounting for properties in terms of fairly uncontroversial entities – classes – and in doing so it gives a clear account of the nature of properties.

5.3.1   Classes and Aggregates

There are a few issues with this proposal, but we should start by thinking a bit more carefully about whether classes are quite as ontologically innocent as they seem. It is important to note that a class cannot simply be considered as the aggregate of all the objects that are members of that class. There is a number of reasons for this, and a powerful one is described by Armstrong as follows:

if *a* is a member of a class, and that class is a member of a wider class, *a* is not necessarily a member of that wider class . . . But if *a* is a part of an aggregate, and that aggregate is part of a larger aggregate, *a* must be part of the wider aggregate. (Armstrong 1978a: 32)

To illustrate this, Armstrong gives the example of soldiers and armies. Take *a* to be a member of the class of soldiers. Armies are composed of soldiers, so the class of soldiers will be a member of the wider class of armies; but it does not follow from this that *a* is a member of the class of armies. However, if *a* is part of the aggregate of soldiers and the aggregate of soldiers is part of the aggregate of armies, then it is unavoidable that *a* is part of the aggregate of armies. Evidently, if properties were identified with aggregates, then this would mean that the property of being a soldier is the same as the property of being an army, which cannot be right. Thus the class nominalist should hold classes to be distinct from aggregates, and she should identify properties with the former.

What this means is that class nominalism cannot simply operate with an ontology of objects only: at the very least it needs to posit classes *in addition* to the objects that are members of the classes. Now, the prevailing view of classes is that – if they exist at all – they exist *abstractly* (they are not concrete physical entities existing in space and time), much the same way in which numbers exist, if they are taken to exist. This means that the class nominalist has to admit the existence of (probably abstract) classes and is by no means free of substantive ontological commitments. However, it is worth noting that this is a commitment not restricted to those who are class nominalists, as many philosophers hold that commitment to classes of this sort is unavoidable, primarily due to considerations in the philosophy of mathematics. Thus, while the commitment is substantive, it is perhaps not too controversial.

5.3.2   Regress

Secondly: is class nominalism subject to a vicious regress? According to Armstrong, it is. This is because the view is committed to the claim:

(CL)   An object, a, has the property, F, iff a is a member of the class of Fs.

It should be clear that we can generate an analogue of the relation regress for predicate/concept nominalism here by considering the relation of being a member of, the problem being very much like the one with the relation of falling under that we discussed above.

However, Lewis's considerations that helped out predicate/concept nominalism can also help out class nominalism. What the regress shows, the class nominalist can claim, is that the relation of being a member of must be taken to be primitive if the view is to succeed. Again, we must consider whether taking it to be primitive is a cost the theory has to bear; but, if it is, then it can be weighed in a cost/benefit analysis, which is preferable to having the regress destroy the theory off the bat.

5.3.3   Possible Objects

With this in mind, we can note some of the main features of properties on this view. Given that classes can be formed with only one member, we can have properties that are only possessed by one object. Empty classes are still classes, so there can be properties that are not instantiated at all. As properties are individuated by the members of a class, two classes with identical members will be identical properties. Also, putting these last two features together, any empty classes will be the same property, for they will share the same members (none).

These last two features can cause some problems, though. Firstly, if we are only considering actually existing objects as members of classes, then properties are extremely coarse-grained. To take the standard example, it is the case that every actual creature that has a heart also has a kidney. Or, to put the point in more technical terms, every actual *cordate* creature is also *renate*. Thus the class of actual cordate objects will be identical to the class of actual renate objects, and thus, on this view of properties, the property of having a heart will be identical to the property of having a kidney. However, this just seems wrong: the properties are different. Also, as we noted above, all empty classes will yield the same property.

Thus the property of being a unicorn will be identical to the property of being a minotaur – but, again, these seem to be different properties, even though neither is instantiated in the actual world.

One way to get around these problems, suggested by David Lewis (1983, 1986b), is to consider not just actual, but also *possible* objects to be the members of a class. Lewis is, in his own terminology, a 'modal realist', which means that he thinks that possible worlds exist in the same concrete fashion as the actual world – the word 'actual' serving just as an indexical, to indicate, when using it, that we are talking about entities that exist in *this* world (the one we inhabit) and not about entities in other worlds. Given this view, Lewis is free to consider the inhabitants of all possible worlds to be objects in just the same sense in which the objects in this world are objects; and he can thus consider them to be members of classes in the same sense. For Lewis, then, classes are made up not just of actual, but also of possible objects. With this in mind we can address the problems we just noted. While it is true in the *actual* world that all creatures with hearts also have kidneys, there are other possible worlds where they diverge: there are possible creatures that have hearts but lack kidneys, and vice versa. This means that the class of creatures (including possible creatures) with hearts *does* differ from the class of creatures with kidneys, so the properties are not the same. Similar moves can be made with classes that are empty in the actual world. While in the actual world there are no unicorns and no minotaurs, there are possible worlds where unicorns *do* exist, and there are possible worlds where mino-taurs *do* exist. Moreover, the class of possible objects that are unicorns differs from the class of possible objects that are minotaurs. Hence, again, the properties can be separated.

However, things are not so rosy when we consider classes that *necessarily* have the same members, or classes that are *necessarily* empty. For example, consider the properties of being triangular (having three angles) and trilateral (having three sides). Given geometrical considerations, we cannot have a case of an object that has just three angles but does not have just three sides. This means that the class of trian-gular objects will be the same as the class of trilateral objects *in all possible worlds*. Thus we cannot get the distinction between triangularity and trilaterality in the same way as we got the distinction between cordate and renate. Indeed, it looks as though the view does not have the resources to say that these classes with necessarily the same members can give us different properties. We get the same problem with classes that are necessarily empty. Consider for example the class of round squares and the class of hexagonal pentangles. These are both necessarily empty: in no possible worlds are there objects that are round squares or objects that are hexagonal pentangles. So we don't seem to be able to say that they are nevertheless different properties, as the classes necessarily share the same members: none.[3]

These, then, are some initial disadvantages of the view that properties are classes. Firstly, the view seems to need to adopt a controversial thesis on possible objects[4] in order to solve the problem of classes that actually have the same (or no) members, and, secondly, even with that amendment, the problem of classes that necessarily have the same (or no) members seems to remain.

5.3.4 Abundance

We can now turn to assess the other features of the view that properties are classes, and note the similarities and differences between class nominalism and predicate/concept nominalism. Firstly, let's take the issue of abundance. Class nominalism, like predicate/concept nominalism, holds that properties are abundant. In fact, it holds that properties are *more* abundant than predicate/concept nominalism. This is because predicate/concept nominalism relies on the construction of a predicate/concept to yield a property, and thus the number of properties is limited by the number of predicates/concepts, which, of course, is limited by the language or thought of human beings. Class nominalism has no such limitations, though. Because properties are taken to be classes and classes do not depend on language or thought, there are as many classes as there are ways for objects to be classified, which, as Lewis notes, is potentially infinite:

> Any class of things, be it ever so gerrymandered and miscel-laneous and indescribable in thought and language, and be it

ever so superfluous in characterizing the world, is nevertheless a property. (Lewis 1983: 346/1997: 191)

According to class nominalism, then, properties are highly abundant – although, as we will see in the next chapter, Lewis himself offers a more sophisticated version, which attempts to reconcile class nominalism with the thought that properties can take on heavyweight metaphysical tasks.

5.3.5   Mind-Independence

Because classes are taken to be abstract, class nominalism can say that its classes exist mind-independently, following on from the account of abstractness we considered in Chapter 2. This feature can enable class nominalism to avoid some of the objections we noted against predicate/concept nominalism. For example, we can say that a heated object's shift from being cold to being hot has nothing to do with language users: as the object is heated, it ceases (at some point) to be a member of the class of cold objects and becomes a member of the class of hot objects; and this has nothing to do with our language or our concepts.

Nevertheless, despite its own distancing from the construction element of predicate/concept nominalism, class nominalism seems to be subject to some of the other objections that are raised to predicate/concept nominalism. Firstly, following on from the abundance feature, we can notice that class nominalism seems *even more* objectionable to those who think that properties should be those things that, for example, mark genuine similarities between objects. There is no such restriction on basic class nominalism: on this view the property of being human or metallic or red is just as legitimate as the property of being human, as both are legitimate classes. This, again, is too much for some to swallow.

5.3.6   Explanation

Class nominalism also seems subject to the direction of explanation complaint, although in a slightly different form from the complaint against predicate/concept nominalism. Class nominalism takes it that objects form classes; but what *makes* a particular class have the members it does? Class nominalism has no answer to this, which is why the property of being human is no more privileged than the property of being metallic or red: these are just two of the innumerable ways in which objects can be classified, and there *is nothing* that explains why the members of a class are members of that class – it is just arbitrary selection. This leads some to think that, as a theory of properties, the view is inadequate. In particular, it cannot explain why we take to fixating on some classes more than others, or, perhaps more substantively, why some classes mark more genuine similarities between their members than others.

While class nominalism may be inadequate as the sole account of properties, it may have more promise, when combined with other views, to form a pluralist account of properties. Indeed, as we will see in the next chapter, class nominalism has been influentially developed along these lines by David Lewis, who aims to make distinctions *within* the classes posited by class nominalism – in particular the distinction between *natural* and *abundant* classes – in order to meet some of the objections we have noted.

5.4 Mereological Nominalism

Class nominalism attempts to reduce properties to classes or sets. However, as we saw, this is not entirely uncontroversial, as classes or sets are usually taken to be *abstract* entities. Mereological nominalism also attempts a reduction, but it avoids classes or sets in favour of reducing properties to *objects*. The claim is simply that a property is identical to a fusion of objects. Or, as Armstrong (1978a: 35) puts it:

(MN)   a is F because it is a bit of the great F thing.

In other words, the property of being red, for example, is just the fusion of all the red objects.[5] Each red object is thus a *part* of the property of being red. Before going any further we can note that mereological nominalism, like all of its nominalist counterparts, is required to take a primitive. Here the primitive will be the relation 'is a part of'. This is because something's having a property is a matter of it being part of something else. Being a part of is a relation, and, if we treat the analysis to be general and to apply to relations too, then two things instantiating the relation of being a part of will consist in their being a part of the relation of being a part of. From here we can see that a regress analogous to the regresses for the relations of falling under and of being a member of can be constructed.

This does not count as a major strike against the view, as all of its competitors are required to take something as primitive. However, as was the case with class nominalism, some fairly substantial – and controversial – metaphysical theses need to be granted off the bat for this view to get off the ground. In fact, mereological nominalism may have the most controversial metaphysical theses of all.

5.4.1   Mereological Universalism

First of all, the mereological nominalist needs to adopt *mereological universalism*. That is, she needs to accept the view that an object can be formed through the fusion of any (two or more) objects. These objects need not be connected in any significant way; they can be as disparate as a London bus and a matador's flag. Indeed, it is crucial for mereological nominalism that they are so, for a London bus and a matador's flag must both be part of the fusion of all red objects, which is the fusion that is identified with the property of being red.

This view claims to have the benefits of reduction, in that it accounts for properties in terms of objects. Note, however, that the concept of object here is not an uncontroversial one, and the objects that are identified with properties are not the standard, singly-located objects we have discussed so far. They are objects that have multiple (sometimes countless) parts, which are distributed over a wide range of space–time points. The object composed of all the red objects, for example, is located at each place where there is a red object. One is thus entitled to ask whether this represents a satisfactory reduction: aren't these mereological sum objects just as odd and controversial as universals are thought to be? If this is the case, then the view does not seem to represent a parsimonious alternative to universals after all.

5.4.2 Possible Objects

The view also seems open to one of the objections adduced to class nominalism. Recall that class nominalists need to posit possible as well as actual objects as members of their classes. This is because there are actually coextensive properties, such as being cordate and being renate, and without possible objects we cannot say that these properties are distinct, because the actual classes share the same members. But now consider mereological nominalism, which holds that the things that share a property are the parts of the fusion that is identified with the property. If we just consider actual objects, then the fusion that is identified with the property of being renate will be exactly the same fusion as the one that is identified with the property of being cordate: each will be composed of exactly the same objects. But the mereological nominalist, like all others, will want to hold that they are distinct properties. The only way to do this, it seems, is to admit *possible* objects as components of the fusions, which would then make the property of being cordate distinct from the property of being renate, as the two fusions would not share exactly the same (actual and possible) objects as parts. So mereological nominalism shares the commitment to *possibilia* that class nominalism has.

5.4.3 Abundance

Properties will also be highly abundant on the mereological nominalist view. There will be as many properties as there are fusions of objects, and, given unrestricted composition, there is no principled restriction on what fusions are acceptable. The fusion of Big Ben and my left foot will be a composite object, and identified with a property: the property of being either Big Ben or my left foot.

5.4.4   Priority Monism

Some more specific concerns bring out additional commitments of the view. As we noted above with regard to predicate, concept, and class nominalism, there are issues of ontological priority. In particular, all of these views are open to the charge that they misrepresent the direction of explanation with respect to an object's possessing a particular property. As Armstrong (1978a: 35) notes, such a charge can also be pressed here. This stems from the basic thought that wholes depend on their parts: the nature of an object depends on the way it is constituted. A whole object would be different, the thought goes, if it had different parts. I would have different properties, for example, if my left foot were larger than it is. If this thought carries over into mereological nominalism, then the whole objects that constitute properties should be dependent on the particular objects that compose them: thus the fusion of red objects would be dependent, in part, on the nature of the individual red London buses and red matador flags that compose it. However, consider again the mereological nominalist's thesis, and you will see that their view runs counter to this thought. This is because the property of being red is the fusion of red objects, and a particular object's possession of this property is explained by its being a part of this fusion. Thus a London bus is red *because* it is a part of the red fusion, and a matador's flag is red *because* it is a part of the red fusion. This seems to get the dependency backwards: surely a London bus in part constitutes the red fusion *because* it is red, and not vice versa?

However, mereological nominalism can attempt to meet these worries by adopting a particular metaphysical thesis. These objections are based on the view that parts are prior to the whole, which, as noted above, may seem to be an intuitive standpoint. But the mereological nominalist can respond if she abandons this view in favour of what is called *priority monism*: the view that the whole is prior to its parts.[6] If this view is adopted, then the charge of faulty dependency can be met. This view is controversial, but it has been growing in supporters in recent years (see, e.g. Schaffer 2009, 2010a, 2010b, Cameron 2010). Whatever the outcome of this debate, it should be clear that mereological nominalism needs to adopt some controversial principles if it is to be a viable view.

5.5   Resemblance Nominalism

In much of our discussion so far we have been assuming that one key role of properties is to explain resemblances between objects. Indeed, we took this to be one of the key features of properties outlined in Chapter 1: that properties are the kinds of things that ground genuine similarities between objects. This perspective takes properties to be somewhat more basic than resemblances, as properties are invoked to explain resemblances. One form of nominalism, though, *resemblance nominalism*, turns this idea on its head. It claims that what makes an object have a particular property is the fact that it resembles certain other objects. For example, what makes a crimson object have the property of being crimson is the fact that it resembles other crimson objects. Perhaps the most prominent contemporary defender of the view, Gonzalo Rodriguez-Pereyra, puts it like this:

> Resemblance Nominalists, like most other philosophers, acknowledge the fact that particulars resemble each other if and only if they share properties, but they explain particulars' properties in terms of particulars' resemblances. They say, roughly, that for a particular a to have property F is for it to resemble all other F-particulars and for it to have the property G is for it to resemble all G-particulars and so on. Thus a particular can have many different properties by resembling many different groups of particulars. Different properties are had in virtue of resembling different particulars. (Rodriguez-Pereyra 2001: 396)

This reverses the direction of explanation we have been working with so far. The resemblance between two objects is not explained in terms of them sharing a property, rather their sharing a property is explained in terms of their resembling each other. On this view, resemblance comes first, properties come after. Such a view is a form of nominalism because it denies the existence of universals or tropes: no additional entities are needed to explain why two particulars share a property other than the particulars themselves (or, more carefully, the *class* of the particulars themselves), and the resemblance between them.

5.5.1 Primitive Resemblance

The most obvious question to ask about resemblance nominalism is how it explains the resemblance between objects in the absence of being able to invoke properties. An initial answer to this question is provided by Rodriguez-Pereyra, who says:

> The relation of resemblance invoked by the Resemblance Nominalist is primitive, in the sense that Resemblance Nominalism does not account for facts of resemblance in terms of any other, more basic kinds of facts. If a and b resemble each other, there is no other fact about them, except that they are a and b, in virtue of which they resemble, or that explains or accounts for their resemblance . . . Resemblance Nominalists cannot explain the resemblance between particulars in terms of their properties, because they explain particulars' properties in terms of their resemblances. (Rodriguez-Pereyra 2001: 396–7)

So, on this view, the resemblance between objects, which we took to require the positing of properties in order to be itself explained, is simply held to be an unexplainable, primitive fact. The resemblance between a rose and a London bus is not something that admits of substantial explanation. This is an issue that we will return to shortly.

5.5.2 Russell's Regress

Perhaps the most famous objection to resemblance nominalism is a version of the regress problem we encountered in Chapters 2 and 3, and this is the regress commonly known as 'Russell's regress'. Here it is, in Russell's own words:

> If we wish to avoid the universals whiteness and triangularity, we shall choose some particular patch of white or some

particular triangle, and say that anything is white or a triangle
if it has the right sort of resemblance to our chosen particular.
But then the resemblance required will have to be a universal.
Since there are many white things, the resemblance must hold
between many pairs of particular white things; and this is the
characteristic of a universal. It will be useless to say that there
is a different resemblance for each pair, for then we shall have
to say that these resemblances resemble each other, and thus
at last we shall be forced to admit resemblance as a universal.
The relation of resemblance, therefore, must be a true universal. And having being forced to admit this universal, we find
that it is no longer worth while to invent difficult and implausible theories to avoid the admission of such universals as
whiteness and triangularity. (Russell 1967: 55/1997: 48)

The basic idea is that properties are to be explained by resemblances between objects. But what about the resemblance
relations themselves? They seem to be relations, in which case
(assuming the same analysis holds for relations as it does for
properties), a relation's being a resemblance relation will
consist in its resembling another resemblance relation. Now
we can see how we get a structurally similar regress to
the resemblance regresses we encountered in Chapters 2
and 3. Consider *resemblance* as a relation that holds between
two particulars. The rose *resembles* the London bus, and –
according to resemblance nominalism – this is why it has the
property of being crimson. We can write the pair {rose,
London bus}, and say that {rose, London bus} instantiates the
relation *resemblance*. How do we do this? For something to
instantiate a relation of resemblance is for that particular
instance of the relation to resemble another relation of resemblance; so we will have to say that {rose, London bus} *resembles* another resemblance relation. But notice that, to do this,
we have to have a new pair, consisting of the pair {rose,
London bus} and the relation of resemblance – {{rose, London
bus}, resemblance} – which instantiates the relation *resemblance* by resembling the other resemblance relation. However,
if we are to avoid circularity, we cannot have it that this
resemblance relation is the same as the resemblance relation
in the new pair, so we have to hold that this new relation of
resemblance is of a different level from (or 'higher order'
than) the initial relation of resemblance. To illustrate this we

will mark it as resemblance$_2$. But notice that the problem does not end here because, to say that the new pair instantiates the relation of resemblance, we have to say that it resembles the relation resemblance$_2$. Again, though, on pain of circularity, in order to say *this*, we now need a new pair {{{<u>rose, London bus</u>}, resemblance}, <u>resemblance$_2$</u>}, which instantiates the relation *resemblance* by resembling an even higher-order resemblance relation, *resemblance$_3$*. But this will yield a *further* pair, {{{<u>rose, London bus</u>}, {resemblance}, <u>resemblance$_2$</u>}, <u>resemblance$_3$</u>}, which will need to resemble the even-higher order relation *resemblance$_4$*, and so on, ad infinitum.

Russell claimed that the only way out of this regress was to admit that resemblance is a universal, which would be counter to the resemblance nominalist's claim that there are no universals. Rodriguez-Pereyra (2001, 2002), though, offers a different direction. His solution is to deny that there are any such things as resemblances, and to hold that all there is are particulars that resemble each other. The fact that we use sentences such as 'there is a resemblance between roses and London buses' does not mean that we must think that there *are* such things as resemblances. Using a strategy we examined in Chapter 4, the resemblance nominalist can *paraphrase* such sentences to show that what they really mean is something like 'roses resemble London buses'. The thought thus is that the truth of the latter sentence just requires the existence of roses and London buses, and not the existence of a resemblance between them. As Rodriguez-Pereyra puts it:

> What then makes it true that a and b resemble each other? The Resemblance Nominalist's answer is: just a and b together. In general any two resembling entities x and y (whether they are particulars or ordered n-tuples) resemble each other in virtue of being the entities they are. If a and b resemble each other then they do so because of their being the entities they are, and so a and b are the sole truthmakers of 'a and b resemble each other'. There is then no need to postulate extra entities to account for facts of resemblance: the resembling entities suffice to account for them. And so no regress of resemblances arises, since there are only resembling particulars and no resemblances at all. (Rodriguez-Pereyra 2002: 115)

As we have noted, the strategy here is reminiscent of the strategy pursued by the 'ostrich nominalist' we encountered in Chapter 4. The strategy there was to paraphrase away seemingly problematic commitments (to properties in the case of ostrich nominalism, to resemblances in the case of resemblance nominalism), and then to show that all that the newly paraphrased sentences are committed to is particular objects.

However, as Rodriguez-Pereyra (2002: 115 note 2) points out, we can register a subtle difference between the two views. This is that the sentence 'the rose is crimson', on the ostrich nominalism view, commits us just to the existence of the rose itself. For resemblance nominalism, though, the sentence 'the rose is crimson' will commit us to more entities, as we need at least one other entity that the rose resembles in order for it to be crimson. Thus, according to resemblance nominalism, the sentence 'the rose is crimson' commits us to the existence of the rose, along with at least one other object that the rose resembles. So the difference between the onto-logical commitments of views is primarily numerical: where ostrich nominalism is committed to the existence of just one object, resemblance nominalism is committed to at least two.

Resemblance nominalism thus holds that it is a basic, primitive fact that the rose and the London bus resemble each other, and hence this resemblance is not something that is open to deeper explanation. We have already noted many times that most views need to accept *something* as primitive, whether it be the instantiation of universals, the resemblance of tropes, falling under a predicate/concept, or being a member of a class. However, one might think that there is a difference between taking these things as primitives and taking as primitives the kinds of things that ostrich and resemblance nominalism so take, namely an object's having a property (ostrich nominalism) and two objects resembling each other (resemblance nominalism). For one thing, the primitives of instantiation, trope resemblance, falling under, and class membership are accepted precisely because of the perceived need to give substantial answers to the questions that ostrich nominalism and resemblance nominalism effec-tively deny that there are substantial answers to. In other words, costs are taken elsewhere in order to respect the basic requirements of the enterprise. From this perspective, the stance of resemblance nominalism is close to that of ostrich nominalism, in terms of giving up on the project altogether.

5.5.3 Sparseness, Abundance, and Imperfect Communities

One interesting point of difference between resemblance nominalism and the other forms of nominalism discussed revolves around the abundance of properties. We saw that the other nominalist views hold properties to be highly abundant, in that their existence is tied to predicates/concepts, classes and mereological sums, which are themselves abundant. In the case of resemblance nominalism, though, properties are tied to resemblances between objects, and this is most naturally understood as requiring some genuine resemblance between objects. Thus, while it seems plausible to say that all crimson things resemble each other and that there is in consequence a property of crimsonness, it seems less plausible to say that all things that are crimson or metallic resemble each other. If this is the case, then resemblance nominalism seems to be less accepting of disjunctive properties, for example, than other forms of nominalism. For these reasons, resemblance nominalism will also be subject to the concerns about determinable properties such as redness, which we discussed in relation to immanent universals and tropes in Chapters 2 and 3.

Connected to this issue is a well-known objection to resemblance nominalism, originally pushed by Nelson Goodman (1966). Suppose we have three objects, X, Y and Z, and suppose for the sake of argument that there are three properties of those objects: colour, shape and texture. Suppose that X is crimson, square and hard; Y is crimson, round and soft; and Z is aquamarine, round and hard. If we take the class of X, Y and Z, it will be the case that each member of the class resembles one another, but there will not be a single property that each member of the class shares: X and Y share the same colour property, Y and Z share the same shape property, and X and Z share the same texture property, but X, Y and Z do not all share a property. Thus we have an 'imperfect community' or an 'imperfect class': a class in which all members resemble one another but do not share any one property in common.

The problem for resemblance nominalism is that the view holds that things that resemble one another share a property; but in this case we have a class of things that resemble each other, yet they do not share a property. Consequently, we have a counter-example to the view that properties can be accounted for in terms of resemblance. The reason for raising the problem in this context is that here we can see that the problem is due to the *sparseness* of properties on this view. If we were to admit disjunctive properties, we *could* say that X, Y and Z resemble each other AND that they share some property: the property of being either crimson or round, for example. Rodriguez-Pereyra (2002: 148) rejects the offer of abundant properties on the grounds that, if they are admitted, members of any old class would turn out to resemble any other, even those that do not intuitively do so – such as the members of the class of crimson or metallic objects. However, it is not clear that this would immediately follow, as there may well be room for degrees of resemblance – which would allow for classes of perfect resemblance along with classes of gradually more and more imperfect resemblance. Thus the class of X, Y and Z, while not being a perfect community like the class of all square objects, would be less imperfect than the class of crimson or metallic objects.

This kind of approach will be explored in more detail in the next chapter, and it looks as though it would be something for resemblance nominalists to consider, especially if they are also concerned about the other problems we have identified in Chapters 2 and 3 for views that take properties to be very sparse; for, if perfect classes understood in terms of strict resemblance are the only classes that yield properties, this will exclude a number of things – for example the determinable properties we examined – from counting as properties.

5.6   Chapter Summary

It should be clear that the project of keeping properties without positing universals or tropes is not a straightforward enterprise, as each of the views discussed was forced to posit controversial entities of some sort. As was noted at the beginning of the chapter, whether positing these entities is better than, worse than, or equal to positing universals or tropes is a matter open to debate. Also open to debate is whether one of the nominalist views is preferable to the others, and this can perhaps also be assessed by comparing the posits of each view.

One common thread to most of the nominalist views discussed, which is in direct opposition to the theories of universals and tropes reviewed earlier, is the *abundance* of properties. On these views properties abound, and there is no principled way to distinguish properties that seem to be more genuine than others. While this feature gives the views examined here some benefits, particularly that they secure reference for pretty much any predicate, it gives them a serious cost too: serious questions are raised about their ability to account for the more heavyweight metaphysical tasks that properties are often required to perform. However, some nominalists are aware of this problem and have offered more sophisticated versions of some of the views discussed, which attempt to make distinctions between purely abundant properties and those properties that are more genuine and do the metaphysical heavy lifting. It is to these views that we turn in the next chapter.

5.7   Further Reading

For predicate/concept nominalism, the main texts are Armstrong 1978a, Chapters 1–3; Searle 1970, Chapter 5; Schiffer 2003, pp. 61–7; Künne 2003, pp. 53–6; and Mellor 1997. For class nominalism, see Armstrong 1978a, Chapter 4; Lewis 1983; and Lewis 1986, Chapter 1.5. For mereological nominalism, see Armstrong 1978a, Chapter 4, and Effingham 2013. For more on priority monism, see Schaffer 2010a and 2010b. The most extensive contemporary defence of resemblance nominalism is Rodriguez-Pereyra 2002, and also his earlier article, Rodriguez-Pereyra 2001. He discusses the imperfect community problem in Chapters 8 and 9 of Rodriguez-Pereyra 2002. For discussion and criticism of his strategy for dealing with the problem, see Jessica Wilson's review in Wilson 2006. 'Russell's Regress' can be found in Russell 1967.

6
Pluralist Views of Properties

6.1 Introduction

On the basis of what we have seen so far, we have reason to think that none of the theories of properties satisfactorily accommodates all the key features of properties that we outlined at the beginning. And it seems that one significant reason for these failures is that different theories do well in accommodating different features. Is there scope for a view that is able to combine the key features of each of the views we have discussed? The views under discussion in this chapter attempt to do just that. The chapter outlines Lewis's influential distinction between 'abundant' and 'natural' properties and explains how this distinction among properties is intended to accommodate the variety of the property features. It also looks at the various ways the notion of 'natural property' can be cashed out, including the use of universals or tropes. Finally, the debate between Lewis's 'graded' theory of naturalness and Schaffer's 'egalitarian' view is explored.

We began the book by considering three different arguments for the existence of properties: the one over many argument, the reference argument and the quantification argument. These arguments in turn gave rise to a set of features that properties are taken to have. We noted these as:

Properties are things that different objects can have in common.

Properties mark genuine similarities.

Properties serve as the semantic values of predicates.

Properties serve as the semantic values of abstract singular terms.

Properties ground duplication.

Properties ground the causal powers of objects.

As we have seen, the extent to which one takes each of the initial arguments seriously may have a bearing on the kinds of features one thinks are important. For example, Armstrong takes the one over many argument very seriously, thus holding that his immanent universals must be the kinds of things that are literally shared by different objects. But he was not too impressed with either the reference argument or the quantification argument, which meant that he didn't see his universals as needing to be the kinds of entities that would immediately serve as the referents of predicates. As a result, Armstrong was happy to prioritise the metaphysical features of universals, in particular holding that their number is limited to the number posited by physical science. However, as we saw in Chapter 4, it is difficult to ignore the reference and quantification constraints on a theory of properties, and even Armstrong himself seems to appeal to them in his debate with Devitt and Quine.

We also saw in Chapter 5 that there is a variety of nominalist views that take the arguments from reference and quantification to be more important to the metaphysical one over many argument. These views recognise the need to account for the meaning of our ordinary predicates, and also the need to hold that properties classify objects; but they pay less heed to the metaphysical need to say that there is something that objects that share a property literally have in common. However, we saw that these views inevitably struggle because of this strategy, particularly when it comes to the question of *why* objects form a class, say, or fall under a predicate. In the absence of the natural explanation – because they share a property – these views are forced to say that such things are primitive, which is theoretically unsatisfying in this context.

Perhaps what this shows is that each of the initial reasons for positing the existence of properties cannot be wholly ignored. The pre-theoretical role of properties specifies *both* metaphysical and semantic roles for them, and any attempt to wholly prioritise one over the other will lead to trouble. This could just be something we are stuck with, and maybe what this shows is that our pre-theoretical understanding of properties is inconsistent: it contains features that cannot be jointly satisfied by the same kind of thing. If this were the case, then the debate between Armstrong and the nominalists would ultimately come down to the question of the features one was less concerned to give up: the nominalists would be less concerned about giving up the metaphysical features, Armstrong less concerned about giving up the semantic features. This would be a somewhat disappointing result, though. It would be defeatist about the ability of philosophical theory to give us everything that we thought a theory of properties needed.

Fortunately there is another path to take. This is the path offered by the views under discussion in this chapter, which hold that we *can* account for all of the pre-theoretical features we took properties to have, provided we are willing to make divisions within the kinds of things we take properties to be. These *pluralist* proposals hold that properties come in more than one kind, one kind being more suited to fulfilling the semantic roles, and the other kind more suited to filling the metaphysical roles.

6.2   The Distinction between Abundant and Natural Properties

In his influential paper 'New Work for a Theory of Universals', David Lewis (1983) explicitly addresses this division in the study of properties. He notes that Armstrong's universals are very much unsuited to be the referents of predicates or abstract singular terms, but that classes of objects are better able to fulfil this role. He also notes that classes are not well suited to play a variety of metaphysical roles, which perhaps entities like Armstrong's universals would do.

Lewis holds in general that properties are classes, and – as we explored in Chapter 5 – classes of not just actually existing objects, but of possible objects too. However, as we also noted in Chapter 5, this makes properties highly *abundant*. As Lewis says:

> Any class of things, be it ever so gerrymandered and miscellaneous and indescribable in thought and language, and be it ever so superfluous in characterising the world, is nevertheless a property. So there are properties in immense abundance. (1983: 346/1997: 191)

The abundance of properties on Lewis's view is mainly what makes for his ability to accommodate the features resulting from the reference argument and from the quantification argument. This is because any well-formed predicate or abstract singular term can be tied to a class of entities that satisfy that predicate or are referred to or quantified over by that abstract singular term. Thus, for any predicate we care to invent, so long as we set out clear and consistent rules for its use, there will be a corresponding property. For example, suppose we invent the predicate 'is conumb' and state that the predicate is correctly applied to objects that are either a cow or a natural number. We can note that, on Lewis's view, there will be a corresponding property of conumbness, which will just be the class of things that contains cows and natural numbers.

Allowing for this abundance of properties satisfies the features of properties that arise from considerations of reference and quantification. Provided that we allow for classes of objects, we will be able to secure a property that serves as the referent for a consistent predicate term. However, as Lewis notes, this abundance causes problems when we want to account for the *metaphysical* aspects of properties:

> Because properties are so abundant, they are undiscriminating. Any two things share infinitely many properties, and fail to share infinitely many others. That is so whether two things are perfect duplicates or utterly dissimilar. Thus properties do nothing to capture facts of resemblance. (Lewis 1983: 346/1997: 192)

In other words, Lewis's concern is that, if properties are as abundant as they are on his view, they do not account for the idea that the sharing of a property makes for qualitative similarity between objects. This is because two objects can share many properties and yet be utterly dissimilar. For instance, the number 5 and Mabel the cow share the property of being conumb that we stated above, but this does not seem to mark any significant feature that they have in common; nor does it seem to mark a way in which they are genuinely similar. So, if we want properties to provide some account of the resemblance between objects and, in particular, if we want the sharing of a property to mark a way in which two objects are genuinely similar, then the simple view that properties are classes seems to struggle.

Resemblance is one metaphysical feature of properties that we noted. Another is expressed by the idea that properties ground the causal powers of objects. However, Lewis notes that here too the idea that properties are abundant classes has difficulty:

> Likewise, properties do nothing to capture the causal powers of things. Almost all properties are causally irrelevant, and there is nothing to make the relevant ones stand out from the crowd. Properties carve reality at the joints – and everywhere else as well. If it's distinctions we want, too much structure is no better than none. (1983: 346/1997: 192)

For example, take again the property of being conumb. This is a property that Mabel the cow has by virtue of being a member of the class of cows and natural numbers, but it is fair to say that Mabel's conumbness does not bring any causal powers with it: Mabel's having the property of being conumb neither adds nor detracts any abilities that Mabel has to causally influence her environment. If this is so, then there are properties that have no impact on the causal powers of the objects that have them. Indeed, given the abundance of properties on this view, there will be countlessly many properties that have no relevance to the causal powers of the objects that possess them. But, if this is so, then we have failed to account for another metaphysical feature that we took properties to have: that the properties an object has ground that object's causal powers.

These failures are reasons that prompt Lewis to look for greater depth in his theory of properties. Evidently we need some way to accommodate both the semantic and the metaphysical features, and thinking of properties just as abundant classes will not do the job. Lewis's solution is to make a distinction between classes:

> It would be otherwise if we had not only the countless throng of all properties, but also an élite minority of special properties. Call these the *natural* properties . . . Natural properties would be the ones whose sharing makes for resemblance, and the ones relevant to causal powers. (Lewis 1983: 346–7/1997: 192)

The first move for Lewis, then, is to make divisions between properties, and in particular a division between *abundant* and *natural* properties. Abundant properties will be maintained due to their ability to accommodate the semantic features of properties, and the natural properties will be used to carry out the metaphysical tasks associated with properties. In the first instance we can still think of both kinds of properties as classes: natural properties will still be classes, but they will be privileged in some way, which enables them to carry out the metaphysical tasks that the abundant classes are unable to do. Thus, for example, objects that form a natural class will resemble each other in some significant way, whereas objects that form an abundant class need not.

By making this distinction, Lewis acknowledges that there are different jobs for properties to do and that we need to consider distinguishing between different kinds of properties to properly accommodate this need: one kind of properties would do the semantic jobs, another would do the metaphysical jobs.

In what follows I will frame this distinction as one between abundant and *natural* properties, as opposed to one between abundant and *sparse* properties. The distinction is commonly expressed in both ways, to mean more or less the same thing: indeed, Lewis (1986b: 59–60/1997: 178–9) first distinguishes between abundant and sparse properties, and then holds that it is natural properties that do the job specified by sparse properties. In subsequent literature the two uses are largely interchangeable,[1] but it is worth noting that they need not map onto each other precisely. For instance, sparseness seems to imply that properties are few in number (or perhaps few in type) – as we have seen in the characterisation of universals and trope theory as theories holding that properties are sparse. However, this need not be the case with natural properties in general. Even though – as we will see – the *perfectly* natural properties will be sparse in this sense, there will be a large number of properties that are natural *to some degree*. This idea of gradation is important to the structure of the view, and it seems to fit better with the notion of naturalness than with the notion of sparseness. Moreover, 'sparseness' seems solely concerned with how numerous properties are, whereas 'natural' seems to reflect some genuine privilege that the properties that fall under the description have (that, indeed, perhaps explains there being fewer of them in the first place). So, for our purposes, we can think of 'sparse property' as being interchangeable with 'perfectly natural property', while other properties – which may not be sparse in this sense – would be natural to some degree.

6.3   Grounding the Distinction: Universals, Tropes and Primitive Naturalness

The next question to ask is what exactly it is that makes the natural classes special. That is, in virtue of *what* do they deserve the title 'natural class'? Standard class nominalism of the form we looked at in Chapter 5 offers little by way of explanation here, as, when it comes to the issue of *why* objects form a class, it cannot appeal to the idea that they share a property – for that would undermine the claim that properties are just classes.

Lewis himself considers a few options here. The first option is to employ Armstrong's universals and to hold that a natural class is defined as a class in which each member shares the same universal. On this view we would have an explanation of why these objects form a natural class: they form a natural class because each object shares the same universal. This would avoid the worry with standard class nominalism, as we would have a grounded distinction between the natural and the abundant classes: each member of a natural class would instantiate the same universal, whereas not all the members of an abundant class would instantiate the same universal. This explanation would also account for the genuine similarity between each member of the natural class: they would all be genuinely similar because each one would instantiate the same universal. The same holds for the causal powers feature: an object's being a member of a particular natural class would imbue it with certain causal powers by virtue of the universal that makes it belong to that class.

A second option would be to use tropes instead of universals. On this view, the members of a natural class would all instantiate exactly similar tropes. Once again, we would have an explanation for the genuine similarity of all the members of a natural class, as they would all instantiate exactly similar tropes. And, once again, we could make sense of the idea that they all possess the same causal powers, as they would all instantiate exactly similar tropes with exactly resembling causal powers.

Of course, each of these options would inherit some of the various pros and cons of each of the more general views of universals and tropes. For example, as Lewis points out (1986b: 64–5/1997: 182–3), employing universals here does not get around the problem we identified in Chapter 2, of having to posit a primitive notion of instantiation to explain the relationship between a universal and a particular. Likewise, in the case of tropes, we still have the problem of finding how to explain resemblance between tropes, which, we suggested in Chapter 3, has to be taken as a primitive.

However, as we have seen throughout, being forced to take something or other as a primitive is an unavoidable aspect of every view of properties, so the fact that these problems are present here does not seem to constitute any additional problem for either of these ways of pursuing a pluralist account of properties. Moreover, Lewis's alternative way of developing the view also has to take something as primitive. That account aims to preserve the main tenet of class nominalism by holding that all properties – even the natural ones – are still just classes. Thus it attempts to do without positing any additional category, such as universals or tropes. As such, this view is 'pluralist' in the sense that it allows for distinctions between classes, as opposed to positing a plurality of kinds of entity. However, the problem of class nominalism still needs to be resolved: what marks out the natural classes as natural classes? – In the absence of universals or tropes, how are we to mark them out?

The answer Lewis considers is one that accepts primitiveness up front and holds that the distinction between natural and abundant classes is primitive: it admits of no substantive explanation:

> Most simply, a Nominalist could take it as a primitive fact that some classes of things are perfectly natural properties; others are less-than-perfectly natural to various degrees; and most are not at all natural. Such a Nominalist takes 'natural' as a primitive predicate, and offers no analysis of what he means in predicating it of classes. His intention is to select the very same classes as natural properties that the user of universals would select. But he regards the universals as idle machinery, fictitiously superimposed on the primitive objective difference between the natural properties and the others. (Lewis 1983: 347/1997: 193)

Remember that the point here is not that *nothing at all* can be said about the perfectly natural classes, it is just that there is no account of *why* they are natural. For example, we can still say about them descriptive things like:

> Sharing of [the natural properties] makes for qualitative similarity, they carve at the joints, they are intrinsic, they are highly specific, the sets of their instances are *ipso facto* not entirely miscellaneous, there are just enough of them to characterise things completely and without redundancy. (Lewis 1986b: 60/1997: 178)

So we can still say all of the things about natural classes that pushed us to posit natural classes in the first place. Lewis's claim is just that we cannot explain *why* they are natural. The user of universals can appeal to the sharing of a universal, and the user of tropes can appeal to the instantiation of identical tropes, but the nominalist view takes it that no such appeal is needed; we just take the distinction between natural and non-natural classes to be primitive.

Is this an unsatisfying move? One might think so, but remember – as noted above – that *all* views of this sort must take something as primitive. Universals and tropes, while they may seem to offer more by way of an explanation in terms of demarcating natural from non-natural classes, must themselves take something else to be primitive: instantiation and resemblance, respectively. All that Lewis's nominalist is doing here is putting the primitiveness up front, so to speak, and not hiding it away further down the theory.

Each of these three options, if used as part of a pluralist account of properties, would result in a theory that required two primitives. Because all three – we are supposing – would want to maintain the idea that properties are classes for the *abundant* properties, each one of them is required to take the notion of class membership to be primitive, as we saw in Chapter 5. In addition to that, each one will take one further thing to be primitive: the user of universals is required to take instantiation to be primitive, the user of tropes is required to take trope resemblance as primitive, and Lewis is required to take the distinction between natural and non-natural classes as primitive.

6.4 Degrees of Naturalness: Supervenience, Definability and Grounding

It is also important to note that, for Lewis, the distinction between abundant and natural properties is best thought of as a matter of degree:

> Probably it would be best to say that the distinction between natural properties and others admits of degree. Some few properties are *perfectly* natural. Others, even though they may be somewhat disjunctive or extrinsic, are at least somewhat natural in a derivative way, to the extent that they can be reached by not-too-complicated chains of definability from the perfectly natural properties. The colours, as we now know, are inferior in naturalness to such perfectly natural properties as mass or charge. . . (Lewis 1986a: 61/1997: 179)

For Lewis, the 'perfectly natural' properties will be properties very much of the sort that Armstrong considers to be universals – the properties at the foundation of physical science: 'physics discovers which things and classes are the most elite of all; but others are elite also, though to a lesser degree' (Lewis 1984: 228).

The most fundamental properties are taken to constitute the perfectly natural properties, and properties are then less and less natural the further away we go from the fundamental physical properties. The reason for this privileging of physical properties goes back to aspects of the methodology we saw Armstrong employ in Chapter 2. The basic thought here is that the physical has priority because everything that exists ultimately depends on how things are at the basic physical level. There is a variety of ways of spelling this idea out, and we will briefly explore the three main ones – through the notions of supervenience, definability and grounding – before also considering the option of taking the distinction as primitive.

One idea is *supervenience*. A set of things, call them the set of As, supervene on another set of things, call them the set of Bs, if and only if there can be no change in the arrangement of the Bs without there being change in the arrangement of the As. One way to illustrate this idea is by thinking of a mosaic (as Lewis 1986c: ix suggests). A mosaic is an arrangement of little pieces of colour which, when seen from a distance, create one unified picture. We can say that the whole picture supervenes on the small pieces of colour, as there cannot be a change in the whole picture unless there is a change in the arrangement of the small pieces of colour. To return to properties, we might think that the world is an arrangement of the kinds of microphysical properties studied by physics, and the macroscopic objects and properties of our acquaintance are like the whole picture formed by a mosaic. On this view, we could say that the macroscopic objects and properties supervene on the microphysical properties, as there cannot be a change in their nature or state without some change in the arrangement of the microphysical properties. This general idea is expressed nicely by Quine, though in a slightly different context:

Why, Goodman asks, this special deference to physical theory? This is a good question, and part of its merit is that it admits of a good answer . . . nothing happens in the world, not the flutter of an eyelid, not the flicker of a thought, without some redistribution of microphysical states. (Quine 1981: 98)

Using supervenience to capture this sort of dependence runs into a couple of problems, though, which we should briefly mention. The first is that it is unclear what the ontological status of the supervening entities is. For instance, in the case of the mosaic, should we say that the whole picture is an entity in itself, distinct from the small pieces that constitute it, or is it nothing over and above the small pieces? The problem is that it seems to be, at the same time, not distinct from them (it really is, after all, just the arrangement of the small things), and distinct from them (otherwise why talk about it as a separate thing that depends on the arrangement of the small things?). We can see this kind of problem arising in Armstrong's discussion of 'second-class' properties that we touched upon in Chapter 2, which he takes to supervene on 'first-class' properties. On the one hand, he says:

To [supervenience] is added the thesis of the ontological free lunch. What supervenes in this strong sense is not something that is ontologically anything more than what it supervenes on. The second-class states of affairs are no addition of being to the totality of first-class states of affairs. And the second-class properties are not properties ontologically additional to the first-class properties. (Armstrong 1997b: 45)

This suggests that we should not take supervenient entities to be distinct from the things they supervene on. However, a couple of paragraphs later he says: 'But it is to be emphasized that this does not make the second-class properties unreal. They are real and cannot be talked away.' This seems to state the opposite: that we *should* take the supervening entities to be things that have distinct existences. So there is unclarity about the status of supervening entities – both in general and in the particular case of the properties we are interested in here. For our purposes in this chapter, we should want the less natural properties to have a distinct existence from that of the perfectly natural ones, but the first problem with using supervenience to capture the dependence of the former on the latter is that it is at best unclear whether this can be had.

The second problem is that supervenience fails to adequately capture the notion of *dependence* we are after. Supervenience is a *symmetric* relation, that is, it works both ways. We can illustrate this with the case of the mosaic again. While it is true that the whole picture supervenes on the arrangement of the small pieces, because there cannot be a change in the whole picture without there being changes in the arrangement of the small pieces, it is *also* true that there cannot be a change in the arrangement of the small pieces without there also being change in the whole picture. Thus the arrangement of the small pieces *also supervenes* on the whole picture. This holds for supervenience relations in general, because these are defined in terms of change between two closely related entities: two things that are so closely related that one cannot change without the other will each supervene on the other. But what we wanted from supervenience here was the idea that one thing *depends* on another: that the picture *depends* on the arrangement of the small pieces, or that the macrophysical properties *depend* on the microphysical properties. Supervenience – used as a surrogate for the notion of dependence – cannot give us this state of affairs; all it can give us is the idea that two things depend equally on each other.

Lewis offers a different option to account for the relation between the perfectly natural properties and the less natural properties: an option that uses the notion of *definability*. He says:

> The less elite are so because they are connected to the most elite by chains of definability. Long chains, by the time we reach the moderately elite classes of cats and pencils and puddles. . . (Lewis 1984: 228)

This would seem to avoid some of the problems of supervenience. Definability does not seem to have the same problems with symmetry that supervenience does, since, if one thing, *a*, is defined in terms of another thing, *b*, the relation will not be symmetric unless *b* is also defined in terms of *a*. Lewis's chains of definability suggest that there would not be such symmetric definitions, though, as *a* would be defined in terms of *b*, *b* would be defined in terms of *c*, *c* in terms of *d*, and so on, until we reach bedrock. It is also less controversial to hold that a defined thing and the thing it is defined in terms of are distinct entities.

However, we might worry that Lewis's claim is a bit strong. Lewis holds that the less natural properties are *definable* in terms of the perfectly natural properties. Thus, as we can infer from the quotation above, he holds that properties like being a pencil or being a puddle are in principle definable in terms of the fundamental physical properties. However, while we might want to hold that there is some sense in which these properties depend on the fundamental physical properties, it is a very strong claim to hold that they are *definable* in terms of the fundamental properties. Leaving aside the matter of how complicated such definitions would be, one might think that certain properties are just not capable of being defined in this way: that we cannot define the property of being a pencil in terms of an arrangement of quark colours and flavours.

A second worry with the use of definability here, noted by Hirsch (1993: 75) and discussed by Mellor and Oliver (1997: 26) is the following. On Lewis's account, to be reasonably natural, a property has to be definable from the perfectly natural properties, in a short chain of definition. Now suppose for the sake of argument that the perfectly natural properties include the properties of being an electron and of being a proton. Notice that we can very easily define the property of being either an electron or a proton simply by disjoining these two perfectly natural properties. This new property seems to be very natural on Lewis's definability account, but it does not seem to ground genuine similarities or causal powers, thus suggesting that it should *not* count as a very natural property. If this is so, though, some revision is needed to the notion of definability Lewis uses.

However, it looks as though Lewis would have a response available to this objection. The response is that the property constructed is *disjunctive*; and, as we have seen throughout, there are good reasons to reject disjunctive properties as reasonably natural. Thus, even though the property suggested is definable from the perfectly natural properties, in a short chain of definition, the fact that it is disjunctive may be enough to override this and place it at a lower degree of naturalness. Of course, this would be to introduce factors other than mere chains of definability into the definition of 'reasonably natural', but perhaps that should have been in place all along.

A third concern with the definability proposal is that it makes the whole enterprise overly semantic. Definability is something usually associated with terms in a language, and it is difficult to see exactly how the idea is supposed to cross over to the metaphysical level when considering the nature of properties. For instance, while we might say that the predicate 'is an atom' is *defined* in terms of the associated predicates 'is an electron', 'is a proton', and so forth, it seems something of a category mistake to say that the *property* of being an atom is *defined* in terms of the property of being an election, or of being a proton. Consequently we might want to look for something that captures the spirit of Lewis's proposal but couches the idea in more suitable language.

An approach that seems to do this and has been gathering steam independently in recent years is made possible by the notion of *metaphysical grounding*, developed most influentially by Kit Fine (2001) and Jonathan Schaffer (2009). Grounding is a way of capturing the metaphysical dependence of one entity on another. Unlike supervenience, grounding is *asymmetric*; so, if *a* grounds *b*, *b* does not ground *a*. Thus, returning to the mosaic, if the whole picture is grounded in the arrangement of the small pieces, it cannot be that the arrangement of the small pieces is grounded in the whole picture (their arrangement would either be grounded in something else or not grounded in anything else at all if it was a fundamental feature of reality). Grounding is also *transitive*; so, if *a* is grounded in *b*, *b* is grounded in *c*, and *c* is grounded in *d*, then *a* is ultimately grounded in *d*. Grounded entities are taken to be distinct from the things that ground them, so, even though with the mosaic the whole picture is grounded in the arrangement of small pieces, the whole picture is itself considered an independent entity.

Given these features, grounding might offer a useful option for understanding degrees of naturalness. One way to go would be to treat grounding as the metaphysical analogue of

Lewis's definability account. The perfectly natural properties will be those at the fundamental base, and they will ground all other properties. Properties will be more or less natural depending on how they are grounded and, in particular, on how long the chains of grounding are from the property in question to the fundamental properties. Given that grounding is transitive, these chains should allow us to hold that every property is ultimately grounded in the fundamental properties. We could thus see grounding as offering something similar to Lewis's definability account, but purged of the unwanted features of definability itself. This new account does not make the strong claim that all properties need to be *defined* in terms of the fundamental physical properties – it just makes the claim that they are grounded by them. Also, at least on Schaffer's version of grounding, this account avoids the unwanted semantic connotations associated with definability, as grounding is concerned just with the nature of things, not with the defining of terms. Evidently there is much room for discussion here, but it seems that grounding avoids the main problems of the other two approaches and thus, out of the three options canvassed, it may offer the most promising account.

The final option we will consider is to revert to a view that Lewis suggested in one of the passages we quoted earlier regarding the primitiveness of the distinction between natural and non-natural properties (Lewis 1983: 347/1997: 193). We saw that Lewis wants to take *this* distinction to be primitive: that there is no substantial explanation available for what it is that distinguishes natural properties from non-natural ones. When it comes to degrees of naturalness, Lewis could make the same point (as indeed he seems to suggest in the quotation). That is, he could say that *degrees of naturalness* are also to be taken as primitive. While we might be able to say a fair amount of descriptive things about what it is for a property to count as reasonably natural (such as that it grounds similarities and causal powers to some extent), no reductive account is available that explains exactly how properties get to be more or less natural. The jury is out on whether this is a good option to take. On the one hand, for Lewis, it seems to fit in with taking the distinction between natural and non-natural classes to be primitive. On the other hand, if the grounding account of degrees of naturalness discussed above can be made good on, then it would make sense to adopt it, as it would offer an explanation in replacement for a primitive in the theory.

6.5   Universals, Tropes and Degrees of Naturalness

What if we adopt either of the alternatives that use universals or tropes instead of primitive natural classes – could we make sense of the idea that the distinction between natural and non-natural classes is graded? Note that it looks as though taking the graded distinction to be primitive is not available to either of these views here. This is because they offer, in terms of universals and tropes, respectively, an explanation as to what separates the perfectly natural classes from the abundant classes. It would be an odd theoretical move to give an explanation of the distinction between natural and non-natural classes, but then to say that taking it to be graded required taking degrees of naturalness to be primitive.

However, it looks as though both views can adopt the grounding proposal, or indeed any of the other two proposals we noted above. Let us take the universals theory first. On this view, the universals mark out just the perfectly natural properties, and let us follow Lewis and Armstrong and suppose that these are the properties of fundamental physics. All of the members of a perfectly natural class will share some single universal in common. If we take universals to be fundamental in this way, then we can perhaps think of them as building blocks: all other reasonably natural properties will be composed of some arrangement of these universals: indeed, this is precisely the move we saw Armstrong make in the discussion of structural universals in Chapter 2. Now, if we want to make sense of the idea that properties can be graded in terms of how natural they are, then one option is to specify that the more natural properties will be properties that require less construction from the original universals.

Let us take an example from Lewis (1986b: 67–8/1997: 186–7) for illustration. The property of being an atom might be thought of as a property constructed from the properties of being a proton, being a neutron and being an election, arranged in a particular manner, with variable numbers of instantiations. In this sense, we might think that the properties of being a proton, a neutron and an election are *more* fundamental properties than the property of being an atom, in that they are, essentially, the building blocks of atomhood. Accordingly, the properties of being an electron, a neutron and a proton are *more natural* than the property of being an atom. In addition, there will be properties that are *more natural* than the properties of being an electron, being a proton and being a neutron, namely the perfectly natural properties of mass and charge, which will be universals. So, with this example, the idea is that the universals (the perfectly natural properties) combine in various ways to form other properties (being an electron, being a neutron, being a proton); and these in turn combine to form the property of being an atom. In terms of degrees of naturalness, these properties will be decreasingly natural.

On this account, degrees of naturalness are understood in terms of structural universals. Of course, on this particular account, the structures will only count as universals if they meet the conditions set out for universals discussed in Chapter 2. The perfectly natural properties will be marked out by the simple, non-structural universals. A similar strategy can be pursued if one prefers to use tropes instead of universals. We mark out the perfectly natural classes by showing that each member of each class instantiates exactly similar tropes, and we limit the tropes to just those classes. We then show that tropes can be combined in various ways to form other properties; for instance the tropes of mass and charge combine in various ways to form the properties of being a proton, being an electron and being a neutron. We can then show how these properties can combine to form further properties, such as being an atom. Once again, though, the structures must meet the criteria for tropes discussed in Chapter 3, and the perfectly natural classes will be marked out by the simple, non-structural tropes.

6.6   Graded versus Egalitarian Conceptions of Naturalness

These pluralist views considered by Lewis all share one significant feature: they hold that there is a gradation in naturalness and that the most natural – or the 'perfectly natural' – properties are those properties that are posited by fundamental physical science. Properties are then more or less natural in accordance with one's favoured account of gradations of naturalness. But it is worth pausing to rehearse the reasons for making a distinction between natural and abundant properties in the first place. Recall that the reasons for making this distinction were to allow properties to carry out *both* the semantic and the metaphysical tasks we took them to have at the beginning of the book. The abundant properties are meant to secure predicate reference even for the most spurious of predicates, and the natural properties are designed for the metaphysical tasks of providing the grounds for the genuine similarity between objects and for their causal powers. We have noted that, on the views we have just considered, the perfectly natural properties are privileged; but it is important to note that properties that are natural *to some degree* also play an important role in grounding similarities and causal powers. Thus, for example, we might think that the property of being human grounds some genuine similarities between objects, and also certain causal powers; but this property is not a perfectly natural property, it is rather a reasonably natural property, and thus we should take care to ensure that we do not just consider the perfectly natural properties when considering the metaphysical tasks that properties do.

This is ultimately why the notion of degrees of naturalness is crucial to a pluralist view of properties. Without it, we just have the fundamental physical properties acting as natural properties, and all other properties coming out as abundant properties. This would not serve at all the original reasons why the distinction was drawn in the first place, for it would leave out of the class of natural properties many of the properties we intuitively take to ground genuine similarities and causal powers, and thus it would undermine the idea that natural properties are posited in contrast to abundant properties to do precisely the jobs of grounding genuine similarities and causal powers.

It is important to note, though, that the claim about degrees of naturalness is separable from the overall motivations for property pluralism, provided that we replace it with something else. For example, Jonathan Schaffer (2004) claims that the idea that the perfectly natural properties are those posited by physical science presupposes that there is a fundamental level of nature, at which these properties are located and upon which all other levels of nature are built. However, it is up for grabs whether there is such a fundamental level; and, if there is not, then we ought not to privilege the properties of physical science in such a way. Thus, according to Schaffer, we can also construct an 'egalitarian' conception of natural properties, where natural properties are all the properties posited by all kinds of science as it gains a scientific understanding of the world. On this view, we would still have a distinction between natural and abundant properties; for the natural properties would be those posited by all branches of the sciences, and the abundant properties would be those that are not. This would still allow us to say, for example, that being human is a natural property whereas conumbness is not; for the former – but not the latter – is invoked in a scientific understanding of the world.

The egalitarian conception of naturalness does need to address the question of what exactly natural properties are. Lewis gave us three options for his graded account, holding that the *perfectly* natural properties could be thought of as universals, as tropes, or as primitive natural classes. Of course, on his view it was only the perfectly natural properties that these options were available for, the less natural properties being accounted for differently. On the egalitarian view, however, the notion of perfectly natural properties is not applicable, as all natural properties are treated on a par. Given this, are the options of universals, tropes and primitive natural classes still available? It may seem that at least some of them are not, as we have seen so far that universals and tropes are just the sorts of things that are posited by physical science, and hence they are seemingly not the kinds of things suited to the more expansive role needed here. However, notice that their role is restricted precisely because their proponents subscribe to some form of the idea that physical properties ought to be privileged. Armstrong, for example, definitely falls into this category when outlining his theory of universals; but, as we noted in Chapter 2, the theory of the nature of universals ought to be at least separable from the question of how many universals there are.

With this in mind, let us consider the universals option here. The claim will be that all natural properties will be identified by there being a corresponding universal for each; and the issue of what universals there are will be settled by the sciences *as a whole*, and not just by physical science. We can seemingly still hold that universals are immanent in the particulars that instantiate them, and that they are repeated in all their instances. Thus, for example, on this view there will be a universal of being human, which is immanent in all particular humans and is literally shared by all of them. However, there is one feature of universals that would make them very unsuited if they were to account for all natural properties in the egalitarian conception. This is the feature that, we said, caused problems for thinking of redness as a property in Chapter 2. On Armstrong's view, for two objects to share a universal, they must be *identical* with respect to that very feature: for two objects to share the universal *redness*, they must be identical with respect to being red. The problem we saw with redness was that all red things are not identical with respect to their redness (some are crimson, some are scarlet, and so on), and hence redness is not a universal. Because of this restriction, for universals to account for all natural properties, it would have to be the case that all properties posited by all the sciences exhibited this feature of identity between their instances. But, as Schaffer (2004) points out, this is implausible; indeed it is part of the very motivation for moving to an egalitarian conception! Hence there is reason to think that natural properties cannot be thought of as universals on the egalitarian view.

The same would go for a version of egalitarianism that incorporated tropes instead of universals. The trope theories we examined in Chapter 3 held that tropes require exact similarity, so any properties that are admitted as sets of tropes must be able to make for exact similarity between their instances. But, as we noted, this also rules out properties such as redness, which cannot count as properties for reasons analogous to those at work in the universals theory. For redness to be a trope, two red things must be exactly similar *with respect to their redness*; but we have seen that this is not the case. As a result, there are no redness tropes, and hence no set of redness tropes, and hence no property of redness. The same will go for any other property that does not secure exact similarity between its instances. Once again, Schaffer's arguments for expanding beyond this restriction the conception of properties posited by the sciences undercuts the ability of trope theory to account for these properties.

If we cannot posit universals or tropes in order to distinguish the natural properties from the abundant properties on the egalitarian conception, then we must trust the distinction between abundant and natural classes to be primitive, and hold that the sciences give us the classes that are natural, but that there is no deeper explanation of what makes those classes natural. Thus we would not attempt to explain the distinction by holding that natural classes are privileged because of the presence of universals or tropes; we would rather hold that the distinction between natural and abundant classes is primitive. Once again, this does not mean that we can say nothing about the kinds of features natural properties have, it is just that there is no underlying explanation available for why natural properties have those features.

So it looks as though the prospects for understanding the egalitarian proposal are brightest on a view that takes the distinction between natural and abundant properties to be primitive, as opposed to making the distinction in terms of universals or tropes. Now we can turn to consider the debate between the graded and the egalitarian proposals. If adjudicating between the egalitarian and the graded conceptions of naturalness depended on establishing whether there is a fundamental level of nature, this would not be a debate that could be settled any time soon! However, we can note that there is room for debate even without settling this question. Suppose that there is no fundamental level of nature, as Schaffer considers: does this immediately lead to the claim that all natural properties should be considered equal? It seems that an extra step in the argument is needed, as we can imagine there being no fundamental level but we still have reason to say that some properties are more natural than others. For instance, in this case it still seems plausible to say that some properties are more basic than others, or that some properties are dependent on others. Consider again the property of being an atom, which we discussed earlier. Even if there is no fundamental level, it still seems plausible to say that the property of being an atom is dependent on the properties of being an electron, of being a neutron, and of being a proton, as the property of being an atom is understood in terms of particular arrangements among these three properties. As a consequence, we might want to say that these three properties are more basic than the property of being an atom, and this still seems to be the case even if there is no fundamental level of nature. Consequently, one might claim that Schaffer's consideration of the lack of a fundamental level does not tell against the proposal that properties should be graded in terms of their naturalness, as there will still be room for the view that some properties are more basic than others.

Perhaps so; but Schaffer could offer a reply on the basis of questioning how exactly we understand 'natural' here. We noted that, when natural properties were introduced in opposition to abundant properties, it was primarily so that they could perform certain metaphysical tasks, namely provide the grounds for objective similarities and yield causal powers. Nothing was mentioned at that stage about the need for properties to be basic in any sense of the word. Notice also that all of the properties Schaffer classifies as natural will perform these two main tasks: being posited by the sciences, they will ground both genuine similarities between objects and causal powers. So all of the natural properties offered by the egalitarian conception will do the jobs that we wanted natural properties to do. If this is the case, then, Schaffer asks, why should we consider the basicness of a property to be a relevant feature for *how natural* a property is; indeed, why contemplate that some properties can be *more natural* than others at all? If what we want from natural properties is the performance of these two metaphysical tasks, then why consider any dimension other than that?

What this reveals is that Lewis considers a dimension additional to naturalness, which goes beyond the grounding of genuine similarity and causal powers. He also holds that naturalness is connected, in some sense, to basicness. In particular, he introduces the idea that the more natural a property is, the more basic, or fundamental, it is. Thus, for Lewis, perfectly natural properties are properties that ground causal powers and objective similarities, and also are the most fundamental properties. Schaffer himself sees a tension in the addition of basicness to the notion of naturalness here; for he takes there to be many properties that ground genuine similarities and causal powers but are not fundamental. The property of being an atom is one such property: the objects that possess it are genuinely similar, and they each have distinctive causal powers, but the property is not a basic one. However, it looks as though there may be a more charitable way to take Lewis's point here. Perhaps we can interpret his view as saying that natural properties must ground genuine similarities and causal powers, and this is what gives them the title of being natural *to some degree*. Once we have an inventory of the properties that pass this initial test, we can ask *how natural* they are in terms of how basic they are; and this is when we find that some properties are more natural than others. At this point the debate between Schaffer and Lewis will come down to whether basicness should be considered a dimension of naturalness *at all*, Schaffer suggesting that it should not, Lewis that it should.

6.7 Chapter Summary

Prior to this chapter we had examined a number of contrasting proposals about the nature of properties, and we found that each had difficulty accounting for all of the features of properties that we noted in Chapter 1. In this chapter we examined a response to this problem, which suggested that we might be able to account for all of the features of properties if we adopt a broadly *pluralist* approach to properties, which allows for different kinds of properties to do different jobs. We examined the most influential statements of this idea – the three 'graded' proposals offered by David Lewis – before considering the 'egalitarian' alternative provided by

Jonathan Schaffer. It should be clear that there is much work to do in specifying the precise details of such a pluralist approach to properties, but that the idea is an interesting one and it opens a promising direction for those who wish to accommodate all of the pre-theoretical thoughts about properties that we discussed at the beginning.

6.8   Further Reading

The main readings here are Lewis 1983, 1984, 1986b, and also 2009; and Schaffer 2003 and 2004. Lewis 1983 (355–77/1997: 201–27) discusses further uses that natural properties might be put to. Additional readings of interest are Armstrong 1989, Chapter 2; Quinton 1973; Bealer 1982; and Swoyer 1996 on the sort of distinction expressed by the abundant/natural property distinction. Sider 1995, 1996 and Williams 2007a also provide interesting discussions of Lewis's notion of naturalness. Work on fundamentality and related issues has expanded rapidly in recent years, Schaffer 2009, Sider 2011 and Chalmers 2012 being the central texts. A good place to start for discussion of supervenience is Karen Bennett and Brian McLaughlin's *Stanford Encyclopedia* entry (Bennett and McLaughlin 2011). For central work developing the idea of grounding, see Fine 2001 and Schaffer 2009.

7
Kinds of Properties

7.1 Introduction

We have seen throughout the book that there is conflict between different ideas of what properties should be. On the one hand, we came across the idea that the primary jobs of properties are to ground causal powers and genuine similarities between objects. On the other hand, we encountered the idea that we posit the existence of properties in order for them to serve as the meanings of our words and help us make sense of the things we encounter in everyday life. On the former conception, properties are taken to be *sparse*: there are only as many of them as our preferred scientific theory needs. On the latter theory, there is room for *abundant* properties: properties that may not be part of our best scientific theory but are nonetheless important for understanding the various facets of human life.

In the previous chapter we examined some reasons for thinking that pluralist views of properties – views that tried to accommodate both of these ideals – might be worth considering. In this final chapter we examine some further reasons for entertaining this view; and we do so by examining some of the roles properties have in other debates in philosophy. The main aim will be to give an illustration of the different kinds of properties philosophers appeal to, and to conduct preliminary investigations into which of the views of properties we have discussed might be able to accommodate them. The overarching thought will be that the best way to accommodate the diverse range of properties we encounter is to embrace some form of pluralism about properties; but the alternative options will be outlined in each case.

The main examples of the kinds of properties we will look at are *mathematical* properties, *mental* properties and *moral* properties. In order to cover these three topics, each discussion will necessarily have to be reasonably brief and only broach a small aspect of the role of properties in each debate. Nevertheless, it is hoped that this will provide enough by way of an illustration of the variety of places where properties are relevant in philosophy and by way of prompting interest in further inquiries in these areas – as directed in the Further Reading section.

7.2   Methodology: Descriptive and Prescriptive Metaphysics

Before we begin, I just wish to make some remarks on the differences in methodological approaches that we have encountered so far, and to note how they may impact on the discussions of this chapter.

Throughout the book we have come across two different perspectives on metaphysical inquiry. We can describe one as the idea that the job of metaphysics is to account for the ontology seemingly entailed by our everyday thought, talk and experience. On this view, it is the job of metaphysics to legitimise the existence of the objects and properties of our everyday acquaintance and everyday talk. We can present the second perspective as the idea that metaphysics should *only* be concerned with discerning the basic ingredients of reality and should not be constrained by what our ordinary thought, talk and experience take to exist. In other words, this second view takes it that the metaphysician's job is to sift through the objects and properties of ordinary experience and to find which ones we should consider ultimately to exist. This approach is not bound by the need to square with pre-theoretical intuitions and can often end in conclusions that would seem rather crazy in everyday life – such as the view that there exist no macroscopic objects like tables and chairs, but just simple particles that are arranged in certain ways (the view of mereological nihilism, for example).[1]

We can call the first view a broadly *descriptive* approach to metaphysics, and the second one a *prescriptive* approach.[2] The former takes the metaphysician to be describing how the things we take to exist do exist; and there is a constraint on metaphysical theory to do this. On this view, it is a strike against a theory if its metaphysical conclusions require the revision of other areas of ordinary thought, or indeed of philosophy. The latter, on the other hand, takes metaphysics to be a more fundamental discipline than this. Until metaphysicians can give an account of what ultimately exists, nothing can be taken for granted. Thus the fact that we seem ordinarily to refer to certain things like numbers, values or colours would not provide an overriding reason to incorporate them in our metaphysical theory; indeed, if our best metaphysical theory does not include them in the list of things that exist, then we should not feel any overriding need to accommodate them.

This difference in methodological approach colours many of the debates in this book. For instance, we can crudely take the approach of Armstrong and the trope theorists to subscribe to the latter, *prescriptive*, approach, and the abundant views presented in Chapter 5 to be more inclined in favour of the former, *descriptive* approach. The *pluralist* accounts of Chapter 6 try to occupy the middle ground between the two.

As should be clear, it is outside the scope of this book to determine whether metaphysics is as fundamental as the prescriptivists think. I rehearse these methodological differences as – depending on where one stands – they may have some bearing on how seriously one takes the problems identified in the debates considered in this chapter. This is not a new issue, of course, as it is one we have come across in earlier chapters, but it is important to bear in mind. As I have noted, I use these debates to illustrate the benefits of taking a pluralist theory of properties seriously. But, in some cases, the problems I identify will not move someone who takes a hard prescriptive line. This is fine – of course, one expects disagreement! – but it is important to remember that there are larger methodological commitments in play here, and that the line one takes on particular issues may have an impact on the methodological approach one prefers.

Now let us move on to consider the examples in question, beginning with mathematical properties.

7.3   Mathematical Properties

In this section we will focus on the problems that occur if one adopts the proposal of properties as immanent universals, or at least Armstrong's particular version of this view, which we examined in Chapter 2. The general thought will be that even those who favour the a posteriori method outlined in that chapter may have reason to consider adopting some form of pluralism about properties if they wish to admit mathematical properties.

We may note that mathematical sentences can take the very same form as sentences about the physical world. For example, the sentence 'the number 5 is prime' contains a singular term ('the number 5') and a predicate ('is prime'). Moreover, it seems to be a true sentence. In light of this, we may want to say that there exists an object that 'the number 5' refers to, and a property – primeness – that this object possesses. Even to say this much, though, is controversial. For instance, consider Armstrong's Eleatic principle, which states that, to exist, a thing has to have causal powers of some kind. Even those who are sympathetic to the idea that numbers exist would not think that numbers have *causal* powers. In fact numbers are often taken to be paradigmatically *abstract* objects, of the kind discussed in Chapter 2. As a result, if we take Armstrong's methodology seriously, we might have difficulty in positing the existence of numbers, or indeed any kind of abstract object.

It is not just mathematical objects that Armstrong's criteria seem to exclude; mathematical properties also look problematic. Consider Armstrong's exclusion principle, which holds that, if a thing can be shown a priori to have a property, then the property in question does not exist. But now consider the number 5 having the property of being prime. It seems clear that showing that the number 5 has the property of primeness *is* something that is done a priori: it is done by showing that the number 5 is divisible only by 1 and itself. This is not a property that we attribute to the number 5 by using a posteriori methods. But notice that, by the terms of Armstrong's view, this means that there is no such property as primeness; for it violates the exclusion principle.

It thus looks as though Armstrong's account of properties, and indeed the general methodology attached to it, rules out the existence of mathematical objects and mathematical properties. This should not be much of a surprise, given the privileging of a posteriori methods to determine what exists; but it does lead to some problems. One problem is how to account for the truth of mathematical sentences, since true sentences that seem to refer to objects and properties are often taken to refer to those properties. There is of course the paraphrasing option we discussed in Chapter 4, which would aim to account for the truth of the sentences without positing the objects and properties in question; but, as we saw, this is a complex and controversial method. Moreover, it leads to a complicated semantic theory, and it does not respect intuitive thoughts about reference. If we could privilege the a posteriori methodology without worrying about semantic theory, this would not be a problem; but we have seen that this cannot be done effectively. Of course, the advocate of the a posteriori method is free to dig her heels in here and to insist that, for the reasons she gives, there *cannot be* any such abstract objects and properties. However, in the spirit of reconciling all the features we initially took properties to have, we can show how a pluralist view along the lines of those discussed in Chapter 6 can accommodate mathematical objects and properties.

Firstly, we can accept that mathematical properties will not be universals, tropes or perfectly natural properties of the kind discussed in the previous chapter. They will not form part of the basic physical features of the world. Indeed we would probably do best to think of them as fairly abundant properties, in the sense that their existence is secured by mathematical practice, rather than think of them as being fundamental (or reasonably fundamental) features of the physical world. Or at least this is how we should take the matter if we consider a leading proposal in mathematical ontology: the 'neo-Fregean' approach of Bob Hale and Crispin Wright (2001).

Hale and Wright's 'neo-Fregean' view was initially focused on the issue of mathematical objects, in particular numbers, the existence of which can be secured, on this view, by examining their corresponding singular terms. Thus Wright states that

> an expression's candidacy to refer to an object is a matter of its syntax . . . once it has been settled that a class of expressions function as singular terms by syntactic criteria, there can be no further question about whether they succeed in objectual reference which can be raised by someone who is prepared to allow that appropriate contexts in which they do so feature are true. (Wright 1992: 58)

This is initially formulated as a general thesis, but we will restrict it here to mathematical objects. The basic idea is that we can secure reference to a mathematical object – the number 5, say – by noticing that its associated singular term appears in at least one true sentence. Thus the truth of the sentence 'the number 5 is prime' is sufficient to secure the existence of a referent for the singular term 'the number 5': the number 5. Here are some more remarks along these lines:

> The lynch-pin of Frege's platonism, according to our interpretation, is the syntactic priority thesis: the category of objects . . . is to be explained as comprising everything which might be referred to by a singular term, where it is understood that possession of reference is imposed on a singular term by its occurrence in true statements of an appropriate type. (Wright 1983: 53)
>
> *Objects*, as distinct from entities of other types (properties, relations, or, more generally, functions of different types and levels), just are what (actual and possible) singular terms refer to. (Hale and Wright 2001: 8)

Again, these remarks are formulated quite generally, and it is a matter for dispute whether Hale and Wright think this holds true of *all* objects, but we can make do with the restricted claim that this is how the existence of *mathematical* objects is secured. The basic idea is that the standard direction between truth and reference is reversed: normally it is thought that the truth of a sentence *depends* on the reference of its parts, whereas here it is thought that, for a singular term, successful reference *depends* on that term's appearing in a true sentence. Evidently this means that, if we take this view on board for mathematics, we cannot understand mathematical truth in terms of reference, perhaps making do instead with a conception that takes mathematical truth to be dependent on proof.

When it comes to mathematical *properties*, the story is analogous. Where a singular term appearing in a true sentence was enough for object reference, a predicate occurring in a true sentence is sufficient for property reference:

> the good standing . . . of a predicate is *already* trivially sufficient to ensure the existence of an associated property, a (perhaps complex) *way of being* which the predicate serves to express. (Hale and Wright 2009: 197–8)

The 'good standing' of a predicate here consists in its having consistent rules for its application and in its appearing in true sentences. Understood in this way, it looks like what Hale and Wright are recommending for mathematical properties is a form of predicate nominalism of the kind we discussed in Chapter 5. On this account, the existence of a mathematical property is secured by its associated predicate appearing in a true sentence. The rules for the application of the predicate could be thought of as being laid down by the associated concept (as also discussed in Chapter 5), the rule for the correct application of the predicate 'is prime' being 'is divisible only by itself and 1'. It will be a matter of a priori proof which objects satisfy the predicate, and hence possess the property. In one sense, then, mathematical properties will be abundant on this view, as possession of them will follow from the correct application of a predicate. But they are not as abundant as properties like conumbness, which we encountered in Chapter 6, since the construction of the rules for the correct application of the predicate is by no means arbitrary.

If we are prepared to accept a pluralist account of properties, then this is one option for understanding mathematical properties. The a posteriori method is respected to some extent, as they are not considered to be particularly natural properties; but they can be considered properties nonetheless, and, while being abundant, they are not *so* abundant as the completely trivial properties.

We have focused in this section on mathematical properties, but we can note that similar issues may arise for semantic and logical properties too. Consider truth, for example. This is something that we may consider a property: we have the predicate 'is true', and we may well think that there is some feature that true propositions have that false ones lack. (Indeed, Armstrong himself thinks this, favouring a correspondence theory of truth, where truth consists in a relation of correspondence between a proposition and the world; see, e.g., Armstrong 1997b: 128–9.) However, we can note that truth, like primeness, violates the exclusion principle. This is because there are many things that truth can be correctly predicated of on a priori grounds – one of which would be the truth of the sentence 'the number 5 is prime'. We can show that this sentence has the property of being true on a priori grounds (by supplying the relevant proof), so, by the exclusion principle, truth cannot be a universal, and hence it cannot be a property. These are negative implications not only for Armstrong's own view of truth, but also for debates about the nature of truth in general, and we might think that a pluralist account of properties has the resources to offer more options here.[3]

7.4   Mental Properties

Next we will consider two cases of properties over which there is much controversy as to whether they can be *reduced* to physical properties. The first is the case of broadly 'mental' properties, such as being in pain, being a belief and being a thought. We will focus primarily on the case of pain and on one particular method: the *functionalist* method (which we briefly came across in Chapter 1). The general thought in this section will be that a pluralist account of properties might come in useful to those who wish to posit a particular kind of property, namely functional properties, which seem to be ruled out by the main versions of views that hold that properties are just immanent universals or tropes.

The functionalist method looks primarily to the *causal role* of a property in order to identify it. For instance, as we discussed in Chapter 1, there is a number of causal roles associated with pain: pain is the property typically caused by tissue damage; it is the property that makes one typically say 'ouch!' when one has it; it is the property that typically causes avoidance behaviour towards the cause of the pain – and so on. This analysis is functionalist, as it accounts for the specific role that pain plays in an organism.

Once we are able to get a complete specification of the causal roles of pain, we get a full description of the role pain plays in an organism. With that up and running, we can then examine the physiology of that organism to find out what exactly is playing that role in that organism. For example, suppose, for argument's sake, that the firing of C fibres is what plays the causal role of producing pain in human beings. In other words, the property of one's C fibres firing is what causes one to say 'ouch'; is what is typically caused by tissue damage; is what typically causes avoidance behaviour – and so forth.

For some functionalists about the mind (e.g. Lewis 1966 and Armstrong 1968), this licences us to *identify* the property of being in pain with the property of C fibres firing. This is because the property of C fibres firing does the job that, for human beings, is associated with pain. In the language of functionalism, it *realises* the pain *role*. In this sense, we have a reduction available, namely the reduction of a mental property (pain) to a physical property (C fibres firing). Moreover, if – as we can suppose – the property of having C fibres firing grounds genuine similarities between instances and causal powers, then we can consider it to be a highly natural property, perhaps even a structural universal. This would allow one who held a sparse view of properties to account for the existence of mental properties such as pain, as the functionalist analysis considered in this way is a programme for *reduction*.

However, there are some obstacles to taking functionalism in this reductive way. The first is that – as Lewis himself holds – mental properties are *multiply realisable*. The basic idea here is that the general causal role associated with pain can be realised by different properties in different creatures. Consider a sophisticated silicon robot, for example, or an octopus. Suppose that by observing their behaviour we can note that they seem to be able to exhibit the property of being in pain, but, upon closer inspection of their physiology, we find that it is not the firing of C fibres that realises this role, it is instead something else, say the activation of silicon chip x3 for robots and the firing of D fibres in octopodes. On this supposition, it looks as though we have *multiple realisers* for pain, each relative to a specific organism: C fibres for human beings, silicon chip x3 for robots, and D fibres for octopodes. This affects our reductive project in the following way. We cannot now say that pain *in general* is identified with C fibres, for this would be false, as, in robots and octopodes, pain is *not* identified with C fibres. Thus the project for reduction takes on a more limited scope: we can reduce *pain in humans* to the firing of C fibres, *pain in robots* to the activation of silicon chip x3, and *pain in octopodes* to the firing of D fibres, but there will be no reduction of *pain in general*: indeed, it seems that we will be forced to say that there is *no such thing* as pain in general.

But now things get a bit tricky, for remember where we started. We set out to specify the causal role distinctive to *pain*, and we found that pain – wherever it is found – has this distinctive causal role, and any property that realises pain must have this very specific causal role. This starts to sound very much like there is some substantive similarity between *all* creatures that are in pain, *no matter what their realisers are*, for any creature that is in pain will have a property that has the specific causal role pain has. But, of course, as we noted above, they may not have exactly the *same* realiser, in which case we cannot say that pain is a universal. The reasons are analogous to those of the denial of redness as a universal: for pain to be a universal, all creatures that exhibit this property would have to be identical *in respect of their being in pain*. But, as we saw above, this would not be the case with humans, robots and octopodes, as each one of these species *differs* in its pain-realising properties.[4]

This has led some philosophers (such as Putnam 1975b and Fodor 1968) to suggest that we should take functionalism differently: take it, namely, to be an *anti-reductionist* project in the philosophy of mind. In addition to the properties that realise pain, these functionalists posit a distinct *role* property of pain. On this view, we consider pain *in general* to be the property characterised by the specification of the causal role of pain, and we state that an organism has the property *pain in general* just in case it has *one of* the properties that realise pain. This would allow us to say what property it is that all humans, robots and octopodes that are in pain have in common: they all exhibit the property of having a pain-realising property. Such properties are sometimes called role properties, higher-order properties or functional properties. They allow us to make sense of commonalities in cases of multiple realisation, as we see here with pain.

For this view to be a genuine option, though, we should note that we need a reasonably permissive view of properties. If we just take properties to be identified with universals or sets of tropes, the requirements on each would prevent functional properties from coming out as properties: as we have seen, there may not be identity or exact similarity between the objects that have the property of being in pain *in respect* to their being in pain, as they can have different pain realisers. So functional properties cannot be admitted as properties if we have too sparse an understanding of properties.

We can note that this is not a problem on the pluralist conceptions we discussed in Chapter 6. While functional properties will not be considered universals, sets of tropes, or perfectly natural classes (depending on one's view), we are able to consider them to be classes, just less natural ones. The property of being in pain, for example, will be the class of things that have the pain-realising property for their kind of organism. Thus, considering our examples, it would consist of all the human beings who have their C fibres firing, all the robots who have their x3 silicon chips activated and all the octopodes who have their D fibres firing. This would tell us what all of these objects share: they are all members of the class of things that are in pain. Moreover, as in the case of redness, we can note that, while this property is not *perfectly* natural, it is *more* natural than the property of being conumb, as there are specific and non-arbitrary constraints on getting to be a member of that class. In order to be a member of the class of things that are in pain, an object must exhibit a property with a very specific set of features, namely a property that realises the causal role for pain.

7.5   Moral Properties

In this final section we will take a look at moral properties. We can note that some of the reasons we had for positing properties in general also seem to apply to moral properties. For instance, we often use moral predicates, say, 'is good', 'is bad', 'is right', 'is wrong', in ordinary sentences such as 'slavery is morally wrong' or 'giving money to charity is morally good'. We also have abstract singular terms that seem to refer to moral properties, for instance 'goodness is opposite to badness'. We also have sentences that quantify over moral properties; indeed, Lewis's example of 'he has the same virtues as his father', which we encountered in Chapter 1, seems to do precisely this. This is not to say, though, that the nature and role of moral properties is uncontroversial, and in this section we will examine some of the main issues. We will begin by looking at the characterisation of moral realism and moral antirealism, and we will suggest that a pluralist account of properties is able to handle these characterisations better than the alternatives. We will then go on to see how some philosophers have attempted to show that moral properties can be identified with universals, before briefly rehearsing some reasons for doubting this.

7.5.1   Moral Realism and Antirealism

Realist views about a subject matter, S, typically hold that there is some reality to S, something 'out there' in the world, so to speak. Antirealists about S typically deny this. In the case of ethics, *moral realists* are typically thought to be those who hold that moral facts are part of the mind-independent fabric of reality and are waiting to be *discovered*. *Moral antirealists*, on the other hand, typically hold that moral facts (if there are any) are not the kinds of things that are part of the mind-independent world. When it comes to debates about moral properties, a crude way of distinguishing between moral realism and moral antirealism would be to say that moral realism holds that there are moral properties in existence, whereas moral antirealism denies this. This would be a reading that would fit with the idea that the only properties in existence are universals or sets of tropes. On this account, only the properties posited by moral realism would count as legitimate properties, provided that there are either distinctively moral universals or sets of tropes, or that moral properties could be reduced to the universals or sets of tropes we are already committed to.[5]

However, reflection on the views of properties that we have considered, in addition to the shape that realist and antirealist views typically take, suggests that we ought to think of the matter differently. For one thing, the distinction above seems to presuppose the falsity of any view that accepts abundant properties; for, if we accept that we use moral predicates, then on an abundant conception of properties it is very hard even for the antirealist to deny that moral properties exist. Moreover, many antirealists want to leave open the issue of whether there are moral properties. For one thing, they may not want their position to entail the problematic semantic commitments that would be brought about if there were no properties to serve as the referents of moral predicates, for example. As Simon Blackburn, an influential antirealist, puts it when discussing his own 'quasi-realist' form of antirealism:

> There is no harm in saying that ethical predicates refer to properties, when such properties are merely the semantic shadows of the fact that they function as predicates. A quasi-realist protection of ethical truth protects ethical predicates, and if our overall semantic picture is that predicates refer to properties, so be it. But ethical *predication* remains an entirely different activity from naturalistic predication, and this is only disguised by thinking of the world of properties as one in which hidden identities may be revealed by the philosopher-as-scientist. (Blackburn 1993: 181)

Of course, it may turn out that part of the dispute between moral realists and moral antirealists boils down to differences in their general metaphysical commitments, the former favouring a sparse theory of properties and the latter a more abundant one. But this does not seem to capture the essence of the debate, which is about how to think about *morality*. It seems preferable to try as much as possible to ensure that this debate does not get distorted by external factors, such as what theory of properties is taken on board. With this in mind, it would perhaps be preferable to have as neutral a theory of properties as possible in the background, on which it would be possible to chart the full range of views and locate the disagreements between them properly.[6]

We can note that this is possible with a form of pluralism about properties that we identified in Chapter 6. On this view we allow for both the abundant properties and the sparse universals or sets of tropes. The debate between the moral realist and the moral antirealist can now be expressed in terms of the kinds of properties they take moral properties to be. The moral realist takes moral properties to be universals or sets of tropes, either because she thinks there are distinctive moral universals or sets of tropes (which would be the route taken by non-reductive forms of moral realism), or because she thinks that moral properties will turn out to be identical with the universals or sets of tropes we are already committed to (which would be the route taken by reductive moral realism). Her reasons for taking moral properties this way would be specific versions of the reasons for taking any property to be a universal or a set of tropes: moral properties ground objective similarities and have distinctive causal powers.

Moral *antirealism*, on the other hand, will be the denial of this thesis. But we can note that this denial does not mean that, for the antirealist, there are no moral properties. For each view (or at least the most viable forms of antirealism) will hold that there are genuine moral predicates and, if we are allowing for abundant properties, this will secure a corresponding property, which is had by anything that the predicate successfully applies to. Different forms of moral antirealism will have different accounts of what the correct application conditions are for moral predicates; accordingly, we might think that different forms of moral antirealism hold that moral properties are natural to varying degrees.[7] For example, views (like some subjectivist ones) that held that the predicate 'is right' is applied correctly whenever the speaker approves of the action the predicate is applied to would posit a highly abundant property of rightness, for there need not be much in common at all between the class of things that fall under that predicate. On the other hand, more sophisticated forms of antirealism (constructivist views, for example), which specified that the phrase 'is right' applies correctly only when it would be applied by a set of ideally rational and ideally motivated agents, might make for a more natural property of rightness.

7.5.2   Two Reduction Programmes

The case for a pluralist theory of properties to make sense of moral properties might be weakened if it were easy to show that moral properties could be thought of as universals. In this section we will look at how two such debates about reduction in metaethics have progressed. G. E. Moore (1903) famously provided an argument against one method of attempting to identify moral properties with natural properties, which is known as the 'open question argument'. While the method Moore considers is not likely to be one that would appeal to a posteriori theorists such as Armstrong, consideration of it will serve as a useful basis on which to consider a more suitable method.

   Moore was working on the assumption that, if two properties are identical, then their corresponding predicates must have the same meaning. Hence, for the moral property of goodness to be identical to some natural property, the term 'good' must be synonymous with the predicate for that natural property. Thus the method Moore considers for reduction would be *analytical* reduction, as the identity of properties is established by synonymy of corresponding predicates. However, as Moore noted, this seems to rule out any prospect of naturalistic reduction for moral goodness, since there is a simple way to show that the predicate 'is good' is not synonymous with any predicate for a natural property.

Let us take the property of being conducive to pleasure as being a candidate natural property for identity with moral goodness. The lack of synonymy between the predicate 'is good' and the predicate 'is conducive to pleasure' comes from the difference between the following two questions:

(1)   Given that action x is good, is x good?
(2)   Given that action x is conducive to pleasure, is x good?

Moore claimed that (1) is a *closed* question, whereas (2) is an *open* question. That is, by the very meaning of the terms involved, (1) only has one logically possible answer, namely 'yes'. The meanings of the very terms involved in (2), however, *do not* yield only one possible answer for (2): it is possible that the answer is 'no'; the meanings of the terms do not settle the matter. This is enough to show that the terms 'is good' and 'is conducive to pleasure' are *not* synonymous; for, if they were, then they would be intersubstitutable in sentences without changing the meaning of those sentences. But the difference between (1) and (2) shows that this is not the case.

Moore concluded from this that *no* predicate for a natural property was synonymous with 'is good', and thus that goodness, as a property, could not be identified with any natural property. Moore's own conclusion from this was that goodness was nevertheless a property, but a non-natural, irreducible property.

However, Moore's conclusion is only as strong as the assumptions he makes, and, as is probably clear, many philosophers – especially those whom we have looked at in this book – would reject the idea that, for two properties to be identical, their corresponding predicates must be synonymous. For one thing, some of the philosophers we have looked at deny the strength of the link between predicates and properties; but, even for those who do wish to maintain a link between the two, there are reasons to reject this statement of identity conditions for properties in certain cases.

Consider for example the properties of being water and being H_2O. Nowadays many people would agree that these properties are identical. However, particularly since the work of Kripke (1980) and Putnam (1975a) on natural kind terms, no philosopher who makes this claim will want to hold that the predicates 'is water' and 'is H_2O' are *synonymous*. This is primarily because the identity between water and H_2O is established a posteriori: it is by doing scientific investigations into the nature of the stuff around us that causally regulates the use of our term 'water', not by reflecting on the meanings of words, that we establish the property identity. Thus, even on views where we maintain links between predicates and properties, there ought to be room for the idea that two predicates can differ in meaning while still referring to the same property.

In light of this shift in the attitudes to the relationship between predicates and properties, a different form of reduction has been proposed in recent years, which applies the a posteriori method of property identification to moral properties. This view, which I will refer to as 'synthetic ethical naturalism' (SEN),[8] denies that there needs to be predicate synonymy between 'is good' and the relevant predicate for a natural property, just as there does not need to be synonymy between 'is water' and 'is H_2O'. SEN also holds that the matter of which natural property is identified with the property of moral goodness is an a posteriori matter; it is not a matter that can be established by reflection on the meanings of our moral terms. Taking the method for identifying the property of moral goodness to be analogous to the method for identifying the property of water, SEN holds that there is some natural property that causally regulates the use of our predicate 'is good', and the property of goodness will be identifiable with that property.

The methodology of SEN suggests that it would be compatible with the theory to allow moral properties to be identified with universals. For instance, in the case of water, we might think that the property of being water is identified with a structural universal: being H_2O. Likewise, it does not seem out of the question, on the terms of the view, that moral goodness, for example, would be identified with a (perhaps structural) universal. That would also be an identification that would be carried out using a posteriori methods, and thus it would fit nicely with the methodology of Armstrong and the trope theorists.

So, perhaps the strongest form of reduction presently available is the a posteriori reduction offered by SEN. However, we can note that there are influential arguments to suggest that such a view would be hard to sustain. The arguments, though certainly not conclusive, give us enough reason to want to be able to consider the possibility that moral properties might need an alternative account. The two arguments we will focus on are Mackie's (1977) argument from queerness and Wright's (1992) argument concerning moral explanation. These arguments are also interesting to examine from the perspective of looking at properties in general, as they give some interesting thoughts on the kinds of properties that moral properties might be.

7.5.3   Against Moral Universals I: The Argument from Queerness

Suppose that moral properties are identifiable with universals, taken in Armstrong's sense. If we match this up with the characterisation of moral realism that we gave in the last section, the result will suggest that moral properties are properties that exist mind-independently: the property of moral rightness, for example, will be an objective feature of the world, just like the property of being metallic. This is one feature that, Mackie notes, moral properties would have on the view we have described as moral realism. So far, nothing doing: we have just described part of moral realism. But now Mackie asks us to consider an aspect of moral properties that seems to suggest some conflict with this idea. This is the thought that moral properties are *intrinsically action guiding*. For example, once I notice that an action has the property of being morally right, this automatically gives me an overriding reason to do that action. There is some 'pull', if you like, that moral properties have: in the case of rightness, the pull that the property has is that, once I notice that an action has that property, I am obligated to do it. But now, Mackie asks, how can a property that is an objective feature of the world and is identified as a universal have this feature? Notice that this is not a feature had by *any* other universal, as bare features of the world seem to have *no* intrinsically action-guiding force at all. Noticing that an object has the property of being a quark, for example, has no motivating force upon the will at all; and noticing that an object has *any* of the universals Armstrong considers to exist has no such force either.

The upshot is that Mackie considers such entities – moral universals – to be 'queer' entities – hence the name 'the argument from queerness'. If Mackie is correct, then moral properties cannot be universals. There would still be scope for conceiving of moral properties in different ways, however, if one were willing to give up on the *objectivity* of moral properties in the sense discussed above. That is, what causes the tension in the argument from queerness seems to be the combination of objectivity with intrinsic action-guiding force. If the former of these were to be given up, and a conception of moral properties that could accommodate non-objective moral properties were adopted, then the argument from queerness would not be a problem. Indeed, this is one way to read Mackie's more positive 'subjectivist' account of morals, where the property of moral rightness can be understood as the property of being approved of.

7.5.4 Against Moral Universals II: Explanation

A second reason to doubt whether there can be moral universals concerns the role moral properties can play in explanation. We can note that moral properties – if they are to be understood as moral universals – must make a difference to the causal powers of their bearers. This follows from Armstrong's Eleatic principle, which places this requirement on universals in general. However, some philosophers – most notably Crispin Wright (1992), building on work by Gilbert Harman (1977) – have questioned the ability of moral properties to do this. The basic thought is that, if moral properties play the kinds of causal roles associated with universals, then they ought to feature in a range of explanations *beyond* simply explaining the moral beliefs that we have. For example, even if the moral realist wants to say that the wrongness of slavery caused our beliefs that slavery is wrong, it looks as though, if moral properties are to be identified with universals, they need to do *more* than that: they must have a more expansive role, which fits with the more expansive roles of universals in general.

However, if we compare the effects of physical properties to the effects that moral properties are capable of producing, there is reason to doubt this. Here is Wright on the issue:

> Let's try an exercise. Compare the Wetness of These Rocks, and the Wrongness of That Act. Reference to the wetness of the rocks can, uncontroversially, contribute towards explaining at least four kinds of thing:
>
> (1) My perceiving, and hence believing, that the rocks are wet.
> (2) A small (prelinguistic) child's interest in his hands after he has touched the rocks.
> (3) My slipping and falling.
> (4) The abundance of lichen growing on them.
>
> The wetness of the rocks can be ascribed, that is, each of four kinds of consequence: cognitive effects, precognitive–sensuous effects, effects on us as physically interactive agents, and certain brute effects on inanimate organisms and matter. By contrast, the wrongness of that act, although citing it may feature in a vindicatory explanation of my moral disapproval of the action, and hence of the further effects on the world which my disapproval may generate, would seem to have no part to play in the *direct* (propositional-attitude unmediated) explanation of any effects of the latter three sorts: precognitive–sensuous, interactive, and brute. (Wright 1992: 197)

Wright's claim is that moral properties seem not to feature in the kinds of explanations that physical properties do. The wrongness of slavery, for example, while we might be able to make sense of the idea that it is responsible for our moral disapproval of slavery, just does not seem to be the kind of thing that could feature in the same variety of explanations as the wetness of the rocks. In particular, its effects would seem limited to the first kind of effects – cognitive effects – but it would not have any of the others. This is some evidence for rejecting the idea that moral properties can be identified with universals; for it is a hallmark of universals that they *do* feature in the three kinds of explanations that Wright claims moral properties fail to feature in, particularly those that directly involve causal explanations. This suggests a genuine difference in kind between moral properties and physical properties, just as the argument from queerness suggested before. If these arguments are successful, then the prospects of reducing moral properties to physical properties look dim, and this would lend more support to a pluralist view of properties, which would allow moral properties to take a form different from that of physical properties.

Of course, both of the arguments we have considered are inconclusive, and debates continue about the nature and existence of moral properties. For instance, some moral realists, such as David Brink (1989), deny that moral properties are intrinsically action guiding, and hence that there is the kind of tension that Mackie advances. Nevertheless, both the argument from queerness and the argument from explanation remain key arguments in the development of moral theory in the twentieth century; and these are just two instances that show how debates about the nature of moral properties are at the heart of debates in metaethics.

7.6   Chapter Summary

In this chapter we have touched upon a few different areas of philosophy, where questions about the nature and existence of properties of a certain kind are paramount. I have gently offered some reasons to think that the pluralist views we encountered in Chapter 6 might offer the best background theory of properties for accommodating the various positions in these debates and the various kinds of properties we might come across. As I noted at the beginning of the chapter, though, just how persuasive one takes these reasons to be may depend on one's view of the place of metaphysics in philosophy. If one takes a strongly prescriptive view, for example, then the offerings of a pluralist theory by way of accommodating various kinds of properties that do not fit with the sparse conceptions of universals and tropes may not be attractive at all, and one may prefer to see instead one's theory of properties as recommending a revisionary approach to the debates in question. Nevertheless, it is hoped that this chapter has provided some illustration of the potential impact of making such a move and has identified further issues to be weighed on the scales when considering which theory of properties is to be preferred.

7.7 Further Reading

For more on the distinction between descriptive and prescriptive metaphysics, see Strawson 1959, Haack 1979 and the introduction to Sider 2001. For a good summary of the neo-Fregean position in the philosophy of mathematics, see the introduction to Hale and Wright 2001. The specific account of properties is given in Hale and Wright 2009 (pp. 197–209). An influential discussion of the tension between a broadly naturalistic outlook and the existence of mathematical objects and properties is Benacerraf 1973. The ways in which a pluralist account of properties relates to treatments of truth is discussed in Edwards 2013b and 2013c and in Wright 2013. For more on functionalism, see Janet Levin's entry on functionalism in the *Stanford Encyclopedia of Philosophy* (Levin 2013), and also Block 1980. Yablo's influential paper (Yablo 1992) relates the determinate/determinable distinction to work in the philosophy of mind. For arguments that favour a reductionist version of functionalism over non-reductionist versions on grounds of property sparseness, see Kim 1998, Chapter 2. Also of interest is the introduction to functionalism given in Heil 2004, Part III. For more on moral realism and antirealism and on the arguments from queerness and explanation, Timmons 1998 provides an extensive discussion. Timmons is also (partly) responsible for a development of the queerness objection to SEN, namely the famous 'moral twin Earth' argument of Horgan and Timmons 1991, 1992a and 1992b, also discussed in Timmons 1998. Lenman's entry on moral naturalism in the *Stanford Encyclopedia of Philosophy* offers a good overview of naturalist reduction projects in ethics (Lenman 2008). Shafer-Landau 2003 offers a broader (non-naturalist) account of moral realism. The naturalness of properties is specifically discussed in relation to ethics in Edwards 2013a. The classic texts discussing moral explanations are Harman 1977, Sturgeon 1988 and Wright 1992.

Conclusion

In this book we have examined the reasons for thinking that we need to account for the existence of properties, and we have reviewed the main theories of properties available. As I noted in the introduction, in the absence of clear knock-down objections to each view, deciding between theories is a subtle and rather complex matter. What we find when comparing theories is a need for careful balance between the pros and cons of each view. Each view has its own ontological commitments and its own primitive notions, and which view one favours may well come down to what ontological posits one finds least objectionable and what notions one does not mind taking as primitive. This is not a straightforward matter, and it may well bring other commitments and views to bear – commitments and views that one has outside of the study of properties. For example, one may not be too worried about a theory of properties that posits possible objects, as one may already favour a view of modality that requires positing possible objects. Or one may not be concerned about positing abstract objects, as one has a view of mathematics that already requires the positing of abstract objects. However, one thing we can do is make clear what the ontological posits of each view are and what notions are taken to be primitive. These are laid out in the table below.

Table 1   Posits and Primitives

Theory	Distinctive posits	Primitives
The theory of transcendental universals	The Forms	The relation between particular and universal
The theory of immanent universals	Immanent universals	The relation between particular and universal
Trope theory	Tropes, sets of tropes	The relation of compresence of tropes; the relation of resemblance between tropes
Ostrich nominalism	None	The application of a predicate to an object
Predicate/concept nominalism	Abstract objects	The relation of falling under a predicate or concept
Class nominalism	Classes, considered as abstract; possible objects	The relation of being a member of a class
Mereological nominalism	Mereological universalism; mereological fusions as objects; possible objects; priority monism	The relation of being a part of
Resemblance nominalism	Classes, considered as abstract	The relation of resemblance between objects

Table 1 *Continued*

Theory	Distinctive posits	Primitives
Pluralism I: classes + universals	Immanent universals; classes, considered as abstract; possible objects	The relation between particular and universal; the relation of being a member of a class
Pluralism II: classes + tropes	Tropes; classes, considered as abstract; possible objects	The relation of compresence of tropes; the relation of resemblance between tropes; the relation of being a member of a class
Pluralism III: classes + primitive naturalness	Classes, considered as abstract; possible objects	The relation of being a member of a class; the distinction between natural and abundant classes

This table tells us what each view is committed to and what it must take as primitive. To evaluate the views properly, though, we must also collate the explanatory virtues and vices that each has. In doing this we can see whether certain ontological posits or primitives are worthwhile in comparison to the explanatory virtues that a theory has. The explanatory virtues and vices of each view are outlined in the table below.

Table 2   Virtues and Vices

Theory	Explanatory virtues	Explanatory vices
The theory of transcendental universals	Accounts for semantic reasons (but only completely if we make the questionable assumption that there are Forms for every meaningful predicate)	Has trouble with metaphysical reasons, especially the causal features of properties
The theory of immanent universals	Accounts for the metaphysical reasons (on the assumption that structural universals are coherent)	Fails to account for the semantic reasons, and success in adequately capturing metaphysical reasons is conditional on the coherence of structural universals, which is controversial
Trope theory	Accounts for the metaphysical reasons	Fails to account for the semantic reasons
Ostrich nominalism	Removes the need for many of the kinds of explanations regarding properties we think are necessary	Is arguably unstable
Predicate/concept nominalism	Accounts for the semantic reasons	Fails to account for the metaphysical reasons
Class nominalism	Accounts for the semantic reasons	Fails to account for the metaphysical reasons
Mereological nominalism	Accounts for the semantic reasons	Fails to account for the metaphysical reasons

Table 2 *Continued*

Theory	Explanatory virtues	Explanatory vices
Resemblance nominalism	Accounts for the metaphysical reasons	Fails to account for the semantic reasons
Pluralism I: classes + universals	Accounts for both the semantic and the metaphysical reasons (on the assumption that structural universals are coherent)	
Pluralism II: classes + tropes	Accounts for both the semantic and the metaphysical reasons	
Pluralism III: classes + primitive naturalness	Accounts for both the semantic and the metaphysical reasons	

Evidently these tables are a simplification of what we have said in the chapters of this book, but they should provide a quick and easy guide to the various virtues and vices of each view and to the posits and primitives that are required to offer the virtues. Which view is, on balance, most favourable is an open question, and the various theorists we have examined in this book evidently make the case for their own views being so. There is of course also room to take issue with the virtues and vices of the views that I have outlined. You might think that some of the vices are not as serious as I have suggested, or that there are ways around them that I have not discussed. Or you might think that some of the virtues are not really virtues at all, or are things that a theory cannot actually make good on. These are all issues to be pursued in continuing this lively debate.

Notes

1 Introducing Properties

1 The one over many problem is also sometimes referred to as the 'problem of universals'. We will use the more neutral 'one over many' phrasing in this book.

2 There is a distinction between similarity and genuine similarity, which is made in order to accommodate the thought that it is possible for properties to ground similarities that are genuine to different extents; see, for example, the discussion of abundant and natural properties in Chapter 6.

3 This idea is expressed in a slightly different way by van Inwagen, who holds that properties are 'things that can be said of things' (van Inwagen 2004: 134).

4 To confuse the matter further, 'nominalism' is also a term often used in the philosophy of mathematics to denote views that deny the existence of abstract objects. There is a certain degree of crossover between uses, if we were to assume that universals and tropes are abstract entities; but I will ignore this alternative usage for the purposes of this book.

5 Most notably Quine, for example in 1960: §43, §44, §50.

2 Universals

1 See, for example, the famous 'allegory of the cave' at the opening of Book 7 of *The Republic*.

2 As Russell himself famously noted (Russell 1905), along with Quine (Quine 1953).

3 Note that Russell's argument here does not seem strong enough to show that *all* universals exist mind-independently; for it

would be fallacious to assume that, because one does, all do (consider for example more mind-dependent properties, like colours or tastes). Differences between properties, and perhaps the different analyses that result, will be explored in more detail in later chapters.

4   Compare, for example, the thought that each individual player constitutes a part of a football team but that, over and above membership of the team, there need not be anything significant that each player shares with the others and that would bind them together as a genuine kind. If there is anything of the sort, it would need to be supplied by something other than their membership of the team.

5   In the *Parmenides* Plato also uses the notion of *imitation*. As Armstrong (1978a: 66) points out, imitation entails resemblance, so, if it can be shown that resemblance fails, then imitation will fail too.

6   This concern echoes Berkeley's (1970) arguments against Locke's (1975) claim that physical objects resemble mental ideas of them.

7   This argument appears in Plato's *Parmenides* (132a–b), as a criticism of the earlier metaphysics of Forms; but the name comes from Aristotle's discussions of the argument, e.g. at *Metaphysics* 1079^a13 and 1039^a2.

8   Russell emphasises this in his influential attack on 'resemblance nominalism', a view that we will explore in Chapter 5.

9   Here and in what follows I will use underlining to indicate each relevant half of a pair.

10   We can note that taking something as a primitive does not mean that we cannot say *anything* about it: we can still describe its role in a theory and the connections between it and other related notions. We will see more of this in Chapter 6 below. See also Sider 2011: Ch. 2 and Davidson 1996 for a discussion of the role of primitives in philosophical theory.

11   However, this is not to say that the view receives no attention. See Macdonald 2005, Bealer 1998, Jubien 1997 and 2009, and van Inwagen 2011 for some contemporary discussions and defences. See also the 'locationist' proposals of Stalnaker 1979 and Cowling forthcoming.

12   These principles are stated in Armstrong 1978a: 113. Armstrong mentions both a weak and a strong form of (2); it is the weak form that is stated and used here.

13   For some criticism of this commonly held view of bare particulars, see Sider 2006.

14   So called after the 'Eleatic Stranger' in Plato's *Sophist*.

15   For more on the determinate/determinable distinction, see, for example, Sanford's *Stanford Encyclopedia of Philosophy* on determinate and determinable properties (Sanford 2011, Funkhouser 2006, and Searle 1959).

3   Tropes

1   There are some forms of trope theory that maintain a two-category ontology, such as Heil 2003.
2   This is by no means a new argument, or an argument limited to this subject matter. For example, as has already been said, Berkeley (1970) launches a similar objection to Locke's (1975) notion of substance, or matter. As we saw in Chapter 2, the issue is also discussed in relation to universals. See, for example, Armstrong 1989: Ch. 4.
3   See e.g. Daly 1997: 157 and Williams 1997: 115–17. Note that the term 'concurrence' is sometimes used instead of 'compresence'. This is merely a stylistic difference though, and I will use 'compresence' here.
4   This regress is also outlined by Daly (1997: 157), who notes that it is a version of Bradley's (1897) famous regress.
5   Ehring (2011: 121–35) considers a variety of other options, but none seems more plausible than the primitive option.
6   A regress of this form is proposed by Daly (1997: 149).

4   Properties Eliminated?

1   Indeed, we will see below that Lewis's 'harder' one over many problem uses a sentence just like this.
2   Armstrong discusses some options in Ch. 13 of his 1978b.
3   However, as Lewis notes (1983: 349–50/1997: 195), there will be some predicates where any form of paraphrase in terms of universals looks impossible. The examples he uses are those of abundant properties, which we will examine further in Chapter 6.

5   Varieties of Nominalism

1   Armstrong himself has since expressed sympathy with this line of thought (1989: 53–6), and no longer takes relation regresses of this kind to be as destructive as he initially thought.

2   van Inwagen (2004: 131–8), who advocates a view which could well be described as a form of predicate nominalism, simply bites the bullet on this, and lists all the features that properties have been taken to have which it would make no sense for them to have on his view!

3   Lewis (1986a: 55) offers some brief remarks responding to this concern, but it is open to discussion whether they are satisfactory.

4   Armstrong says of this that, 'if Class Nominalism can only be defended by embracing an ontology of possible worlds, then the remedy is worse than the disease' (Armstrong 1978a: 36). Lewis, of course, would disagree, and he argues for modal realism extensively in Lewis 1986b. But could the view also work with less controversial accounts of possible worlds, such as abstract ones (e.g. Plantinga 2003) or fictionalist ones (e.g. Yablo 1996)? Perhaps; but then we would need to accept that classes are not simply made up of concrete objects, but maybe also of abstract or fictional ones – and this is by no means ontologically unproblematic.

5   One might wonder if the red fusion is itself red; thus one would be posing a question akin to asking whether Plato's form of red is itself red. Fortunately for the mereological nominalist, there is a quick response. According to classical mereology, parthood is reflexive, so a whole is also a part of itself, which means that the red fusion is also a part of itself; and this allows it to have the property of being red.

6   This option was first suggested by Nikk Effingham (2013).

6   Pluralist Views of Properties

1   See Sider 1995 for a careful assessment.

7   Kinds of Properties

1   See, for example, van Inwagen 1990 and Merricks 2001.

2   This distinction is due to Strawson (1959).

3   As argued in Edwards 2013c. Edwards (2013b) also discusses property naturalness in relation to truth, and Weatherson (2003) and Williamson (2007) discuss naturalness in relation to the closely related notions of knowledge and reference, respectively.

4   It is worth noting that there is room for discussion here. Shoe-maker (2001), for example, offers a different option, which suggests that functional properties are not causally separable from their realisers. McLaughlin (2007) offers a critique of Shoemaker's view, and questions whether such theoretical room is available.

5   Of course, there is also the possible view that even moral realism would not think that moral properties are capable of being universals or sets of tropes. If this were the case, then we would have an even more direct argument for property plural-ism; for, in its absence, not even moral realism could posit moral properties! However, I leave this possibility aside for now, in order to consider the strongest case for property sparseness.

6   For this general methodological strategy as it relates to the case of truth, see Edwards 2013c.

7   One notable exception would be extreme error-theoretical views, which hold that moral predicates are *never* correctly applied, as there are no moral properties at all – on any under-standing of properties.

8   It is also referred to as 'Cornell realism', in light of the location (at the time) of those most associated with the view, namely Brink (1989), Boyd (1988), and Sturgeon (1988).

References

Alston, W. P. 1958. Ontological Commitments. *Philosophical Studies* 9.1–2: 8–17.

Aristotle. 1908. *Metaphysics* (trans. W. D. Ross). Oxford: Clarendon.

Armstrong, D. M. 1968. *A Materialistic Theory of the Mind*. London: Routledge.

Armstrong, D. M. 1978a. *Universals and Scientific Realism*, vol. 1: *Universals and Scientific Realism*. Cambridge: Cambridge University Press.

Armstrong, D. M. 1978b. *Universals and Scientific Realism*, vol. 2: *A Theory of Universals*. Cambridge: Cambridge University Press.

Armstrong, D. M. 1980. Against 'Ostrich' Nominalism. *Pacific Philosophical Quarterly* 61: 440–9. Reprinted in Mellor and Oliver 1997, pp. 101–11.

Armstrong, D. M. 1986. In Defence of Structural Universals. *Australasian Journal of Philosophy* 64: 85–8.

Armstrong, D. M. 1989. *Universals: An Opinionated Introduction*. New York: Westview.

Armstrong, D. M. 1997a. Properties. In Mellor and Oliver, pp. 160–72.

Armstrong, D. M. 1997b. *A World of States of Affairs*. Cambridge: Cambridge University Press.

Armstrong, D. M. 2004. *Truth and Truthmakers*. Cambridge: Cambridge University Press.

Azzouni, J. 1998. On 'On What There Is'. *Pacific Philosophical Quarterly* 79.1: 1–18.

Azzouni, J. 2010. *Talking about Nothing: Numbers, Hallucinations and Fictions*. New York: Oxford University Press.

Bealer, G. 1982. *Quality and Concept*. Oxford: Clarendon.

Bealer, G. 1998. Universals and Properties. In S. Laurence and C. Macdonald (eds.), *Contemporary Readings in the Foundations of Metaphysics*. Oxford: Blackwell.

Benacerraf, P. 1973. Mathematical Truth. *Journal of Philosophy* 70.19: 661–79.

Bennett, K. and McLaughlin, B. 2011. Supervenience. In Edward N. Zalta (ed.), *The Stanford Encyclopedia of Philosophy*, <http:// plato.stanford.edu/archives/win2011/entries/supervenience/>.

Berkeley, G. 1970. *Principles of Human Knowledge* [1710], edited by C. Murray Turbayne. New York: Bobbs-Merrill.

Blackburn, S. 1993. *Essays in Quasi-Realism*. Oxford: Oxford University Press.

Block, N. 1980. What Is Functionalism? In N. Block (ed.), *Readings in Philosophy of Psychology*, vol. 1. Cambridge, MA: Harvard University Press, pp. 171–84.

Boyd, R. 1988. How to Be a Moral Realist. In G. Sayre-McCord (ed.), *Essays on Moral Realism*. Ithaca, NY: Cornell University Press, pp. 307–56.

Bradley, F. H. 1897. *Appearance and Reality*. Oxford: Oxford University Press.

Brink, D. O. 1989. *Moral Realism and the Foundations of Ethics*. Cambridge: Cambridge University Press.

Cameron, R. P. 2008. Truthmakers and Ontological Commitment: Or How to Deal with Complex Objects and Mathematical Ontology without Getting into Trouble. *Philosophical Studies* 140: 1–18.

Cameron, R. P. 2010. From Humean Truthmaker Theory to Priority Monism. *Nous* 44: 178–98.

Campbell, K. 1990. *Abstract Particulars*. Oxford: Blackwell.

Campbell, K. 1997. The Metaphysic of Abstract Particulars. In Mellor and Oliver, pp. 125–39. Originally printed in *Midwest Studies in Philosophy* 6 (1981): 477–86.

Chalmers, D. 2012. *Constructing the World*. Oxford: Oxford University Press.

Clapp, L. 2001. Disjunctive Properties: Multiple Realizations. *Journal of Philosophy* 8.3: 111–36.

Cook Wilson, J. 1926. *Statement and Inference with Other Philosophical Papers*. Oxford: Clarendon.

Cowling, S. Forthcoming. Instantiation as Location. *Philosophical Studies*. Online First Edition published at <http://dx.doi .org/10.1007/s11098-013-0120-z>.

Daly, C. 1997. Tropes. In Mellor and Oliver, pp. 140–59. Earlier version in *Proceedings of the Aristotelian Society* 94 (1994): 253–61.

Davidson, D. 1996. The Folly of Trying to Define Truth. *The Journal of Philosophy* 93.6: 263–78.

Devitt, M. 1980. 'Ostrich Nominalism' or 'Mirage Realism'? *Pacific Philosophical Quarterly* 61: 433–9. Reprinted in Mellor and Oliver 1997, pp. 93–100.

Devitt, M. 2010. *Putting Metaphysics First*. Oxford: Oxford University Press.

Edwards, D. 2012. On Alethic Disjunctivism. *Dialectica* 66.1: 200–14.

Edwards, D. 2013a. The Eligibility of Ethical Naturalism. *Pacific Philosophical Quarterly* 94.1: 1–18.

Edwards, D. 2013b. Naturalness, Representation, and the Metaphysics of Truth. *European Journal of Philosophy* 21.3: 384–401.

Edwards, D. 2013c. Truth as a Substantive Property. *Australasian Journal of Philosophy* 91.2: 279–94.

Effingham, N. 2013. Mereological Nominalism Renewed, <http://www.nikkeffingham.com/resources/Mereological+Nominalism+Renewed.pdf>.

Ehring, D. 2011. *Tropes: Properties, Objects, and Mental Causation*. Oxford: Oxford University Press.

Fine, K. 2001. The Question of Realism. *Philosophers' Imprint* 1.1: 1–30.

Fodor, J. 1968. The Appeal to Tacit Knowledge in Psychological Explanations. *Journal of Philosophy* 65: 627–40.

Funkhouser, E. 2006. The Determinable–Determinate Relation. *Nous* 40: 548–69.

Goodman, N. 1966. *The Structure of Appearance* (2nd edn). Indianapolis, IN: Bobbs-Merrill.

Haack, S. 1979. Descriptive and Revisionary Metaphysics. *Philosophical Studies* 35.4: 361–71.

Hale, B. and Wright, C. J. G. 2001. *The Reason's Proper Study*. Oxford: Oxford University Press.

Hale, B. and Wright, C. J. G. 2009. The Metaontology of Abstraction. In D. Chalmers, D. Manley and R. Wasserman (eds), *Metametaphysics*. Oxford: Oxford University Press, pp. 178–212.

Harman, G. 1977. *The Nature of Morality*. New York: Oxford University Press.

Hawley, K. 2010. Mereology, Modality and Magic. *Australasian Journal of Philosophy* 88.1: 117–33.

Heil, J. 2003. *From an Ontological Point of View*. Oxford: Oxford University Press.

Heil, J. 2004. *Philosophy of Mind: A Guide and Anthology*. Oxford: Oxford University Press.

Hirsch, E. 1993. *Dividing Reality*. New York: Oxford University Press.

Hodes, H. 1990. Ontological Commitments, Thick and Thin. In G. Boolos (ed.), *Method, Reason and Language: Essays in Honor of Hilary Putnam*. Cambridge: Cambridge University Press, pp. 235–60.

Horgan, T. and Timmons, M. 1991. New-Wave Moral Realism Meets Moral Twin Earth. *Journal of Philosophical Research*, 16: 447–65.

Horgan, T. and Timmons, M. 1992a. Troubles on Moral Twin Earth: Moral Queerness Revived? *Synthese* 92: 221–60.

Horgan, T. and Timmons, M. 1992b. Troubles for New Wave Moral Semantics: The 'Open Question Argument' Revived. *Philosophical Papers* 21: 153–75.

Jackson, F. 1977. Statements about Universals. *Mind* 86: 427–9. Reprinted in Mellor and Oliver 1997, pp. 89–92.

Jubien, M. 1997. *Contemporary Metaphysics: An Introduction*. Oxford: Blackwell.

Jubien, M. 2009. *Possibility*. Oxford: Oxford University Press.

Kim, J. 1998. *Mind in a Physical World*. Cambridge, MA: MIT Press.

Kripke, S. 1980. *Naming and Necessity*. Oxford: Blackwell.

Künne, W. 2003. *Conceptions of Truth*, Oxford: Oxford University Press.

Ladyman, J. and Ross, D., with Spurrett, D. and Collier, J. 2007. *Every Thing Must Go*. Oxford: Oxford University Press.

Landesman, C. 1973. Abstract Particulars. *Philosophy and Phenomenological Research* 33.3: 323–37.

Lenman, J. 2008. Moral Naturalism. In Edward N. Zalta (ed.), *The Stanford Encyclopedia of Philosophy*, <http://plato.stanford.edu/archives/win2008/entries/naturalism-moral/>.

Levin, J. 2013. Functionalism. In Edward N. Zalta (ed.), *The Stanford Encyclopedia of Philosophy*, <http://plato.stanford.edu/archives/sum2010/entries/functionalism/>.

Lewis, D. 1966. An Argument for the Identity Theory. *Journal of Philosophy* 63: 17–25.

Lewis, D. 1983. New Work for a Theory of Universals. *Australasian Journal of Philosophy* 61.4: 343–77. Reprinted in Mellor and Oliver 1997, pp. 118–227.

Lewis, D. 1984. Putnam's Paradox. *Australasian Journal of Philosophy* 62: 221–36.

Lewis, D. 1986a. Against Structural Universals. *Australasian Journal of Philosophy* 62: 25–46.

Lewis, D. 1986b. *On the Plurality of Worlds*. Oxford: Blackwell. Excerpt reprinted in Mellor and Oliver 1997, pp. 173–87.

Lewis, D. 1986c. *Philosophical Papers*, vol. 2. Oxford: Oxford University Press.

Lewis, D. 2009. Ramseyan Humility. In D. Braddon-Mitchell and R. Nola (eds), *Conceptual Analysis and Philosophical Naturalism*. Cambridge, MA: MIT Press, pp. 203–22.

Locke, J. 1975. *An Essay Concerning Human Understanding* [1690], edited by P. Nidditch. Oxford: Clarendon.

Lowe, E. J. 2002. Properties, Modes, and Universals. *The Modern Schoolman*, LXXIX: pp. 13750.

Lowe, E. J. 2006. *The Four-Category Ontology: A Metaphysical Foundation for Natural Science*. Oxford: Clarendon Press.

Lynch, M. P. 2009. *Truth as One and Many*, Oxford: Oxford University Press.

Macdonald, C. 2005. *Varieties of Things*. Oxford: Blackwell.

Mackie, J. L. 1977. *Ethics: Inventing Right and Wrong*. London: Penguin.

Martin, C. B. 1980. Substance Substantiated. *Australasian Journal of Philosophy* 58: 3–10.

Maurin, A. 2002. *If Tropes*. Dordrecht: Kluwer.

Maurin, A. 2010. Trope Theory and the Bradley Regress. *Synthese* 175: 311–26.

Maurin, A. 2013. Tropes. In D. Pritchard (ed.), *Oxford Bibliographies*, <http://www.oxfordbibliographies.com/obo/page/philosophy>.

McDaniel, K. 2001. Tropes and Ordinary Physical Objects. *Philosophical Studies* 104.3: 269–90.

McLaughlin, B. 2007. Mental Causation and Shoemaker-Realization. *Erkenntnis* 67: 149–72.

McTaggart, J. 1921. *The Nature of Existence*. Cambridge: Cambridge University Press.

Mellor, D. H. 1992. There Are No Conjunctive Universals. *Analysis* 52.2: 97–103.

Mellor, D. H. 1997. Properties and Predicates. In Mellor and Oliver, pp. 255–67.

Mellor, D. H. and Oliver, A. (eds.). 1997. *Properties*. Oxford: Oxford University Press.

Merricks, T. 2001. *Objects and Persons*. Oxford: Clarendon.

Moore, G. E. 1903. *Principia ethica*. Cambridge: Cambridge University Press.

Moreland, J. P. 2001. *Universals*. McGill-Queens University Press, Canada: Acumen.

Oliver, A. 1992. Could There Be Conjunctive Universals? *Analysis* 52.2: 88–97.

Oliver, A. 1996. The Metaphysics of Properties. *Mind* (New Series) 105.417: 1–80.

Pap, A. 1959. Nominalism, Empiricism and Universals 1. *The Philosophical Quarterly* 9: 330–40.

Paul, L. A. 2002. Logical Parts. *Noûs* 36: 578–96.

Paul, L. A. 2006. In Defense of Essentialism. *Philosophical Perspectives*, 20: 333–72.

Pickel, B. and Mantegani, N. 2012. A Quinean Critique of Ostrich Nominalism. *Philosophers' Imprint* 12.6: 1–21.

Plantinga, A. 2003. *Essays in the Metaphysics of Modality*, edited by M. Davidson. New York: Oxford University Press.

Plato. 1965. *Parmenides* (trans. L. Tarán). Princeton, NJ: Princeton University Press.

Plato. 1987. *The Republic* (trans. D. Lee). London: Penguin Classics.

Plato. 1993. *The Sophist* (trans. N. P. White). Indianapolis, IN: Hackett Publishing Company.

Putnam, H. 1975a. The Meaning of 'Meaning'. In K. Gunderson (ed.), *Language, Mind and Knowledge* (Minnesota Studies in the Philosophy of Science 7). Minneapolis: University of Minnesota Press, pp. 131–93.

Putnam, H. 1975b. The Nature of Mental States. In H. Putnam, *Mind, Language and Reality: Philosophical Papers II*. Cambridge: Cambridge University Press.

Quine, W. V. O. 1953. On What There Is. In W. V. O. Quine, *From a Logical Point of View*. Cambridge, MA: Harvard University Press, pp. 1–19. Reprinted in Mellor and Oliver 1997, pp. 74–88.

Quine, W. V. O. 1960. *Word and Object*. Cambridge, MA: MIT Press.

Quine, W. V. O. 1981. *Theories and Things*. Cambridge, MA: Harvard University Press.

Quinton, A. 1973. *The Nature of Things*. London: Routledge.

Ramsey, F. P. 1925. Universals. *Mind* 34.136: 401–17. Reprinted in Mellor and Oliver 1997, pp. 57–73.

Rodriguez-Pereyra, G. 2001. Resemblance Nominalism and Russell's Regress. *Australasian Journal of Philosophy* 79.3: 395–408.

Rodriguez-Pereyra, G. 2002. *Resemblance Nominalism: A Solution to the Problem of Universals*. Oxford: Oxford University Press.

Russell, B. 1905. On Denoting. *Mind* 141.56: 479–93.

Russell, B. 1967. The World of Universals [1912]. In B. Russell, *The Problems of Philosophy*. Oxford: Oxford University Press, pp. 52–7. Reprinted in Mellor and Oliver 1997, pp. 45–56.

Sanford, D. H. 2011. Determinates vs. Determinables. In Edward N. Zalta (ed.), *The Stanford Encyclopedia of Philosophy*, <http://plato.stanford.edu/archives/spr2013/entries/determinate-determinables/>.

Schaffer, J. 2001. The Individuation of Tropes. *Australasian Journal of Philosophy* 79.2: 247–57.

Schaffer, J. 2003. Is There a Fundamental Level? *Nous* 37.3: 498–517.

Schaffer, J. 2004. Two Conceptions of Sparse Properties. *Pacific Philosophical Quarterly* 85.1: 92–102.

Schaffer, J. 2008. Truthmaker Commitments. *Philosophical Studies* 141: 7–19.

Schaffer, J. 2009. On What Grounds What. In D. Chalmers, D. Manley and R. Wasserman (eds.), *Metametaphysics*. Oxford: Oxford University Press, pp. 347–83.

Schaffer, J. 2010a. The Internal Relatedness of All Things. *Mind* 119: 341–76.

Schaffer, J. 2010b. Monism: The Priority of the Whole. *Philosophical Review* 119.1: 31–76.

Schiffer, S. 2003. *The Things We Mean*. Oxford: Oxford University Press.

Searle, J. 1959. On Determinables and Resemblance, II. *Proceedings of the Aristotelian Society* (Supplementary Volume) 33: 141–58.

Searle, J. 1970. *Speech Acts*. Cambridge: Cambridge University Press.

Shafer-Landau, R. 2003. *Moral Realism: A Defence*. Oxford: Oxford University Press.

Shoemaker, S. 1980. Causality and Properties. In P. van Inwagen (ed.), *Time and Cause*. Dordrecht: D. Reidel, pp. 109–35. Reprinted in Mellor and Oliver 1997, pp. 228–54.

Shoemaker, S. 2001. Realization and Mental Causation. In G. Gillett and B. Loewer (eds.), *Physicalism and Its Discontents*. Cambridge: Cambridge University Press, pp. 74–98.

Sider, T. 1995. Sparseness, Immanence, and Naturalness. *Noûs* 29: 360–77.

Sider, T. 1996. Naturalness and Arbitrariness. *Philosophical Studies* 81: 283–301.

Sider, T. 2001. *Four-Dimensionalism*. Oxford: Oxford University Press.

Sider, T. 2006. Bare Particulars. *Philosophical Perspectives* 20: 387–97.

Sider, T. 2011. *Writing the Book of the World*. Oxford: Oxford University Press.

Simons, P. 1994. Particulars in Particular Clothing. *Philosophy and Phenomenological Research* 53.3: 553–75.

Stalnaker, R. 1979. Anti-Essentialism. *Midwest Studies in Philosophy* 4: 343–55.

Stout, G. F. 1921. The Nature of Universals and Propositions. *Proceedings of the British Academy* 10: 157–72.

Stout, G. F. 1923. Are the Characteristics of Particular Things Particular or Universal? *Proceedings of the Aristotelian Society* (Supplementary Volume) 3: 114–22.

Stout, G. F. 1930. The Nature of Universals and Propositions. In G. F. Stout, *Studies in Philosophy and Psychology*. London: Macmillan, pp. 384–404.

Strawson, P. F. 1959. *Individuals*. London: Methuen.

Sturgeon, N. 1988. Moral Explanations. In G. Sayre-McCord (ed.), *Essays on Moral Realism*. Ithaca: Cornell University Press, pp. 229–55.

Swoyer, C. 1996. Theories of Properties: From Plenitude to Paucity. *Philosophical Perspectives* 10: 243–64.

Timmons, M. 1998. *Morality without Foundations*. Oxford: Oxford University Press.

van Cleve, J. 1994. Predication without Universals? A Fling with Ostrich Nominalism. *Philosophy and Phenomenological Research* 54.3: 577–90.

van Inwagen, P. 1990. *Material Beings*. Ithica, NY: Cornell University Press.

van Inwagen, P. 2004. A Theory of Properties. *Oxford Studies in Metaphysics* 1: 107–38.

van Inwagen, P. 2011. Relational vs. Constituent Ontologies. *Philosophical Perspectives*, 25: 389–405.

Weatherson, B. 2003. What Good are Counterexamples? *Philosophical Studies* 115: 1–31.

Williams, D. C. 1953. On the Elements of Being, II. *Review of Metaphysics* 7: 171–92.

Williams, D. C. 1997. On the Elements of Being, I. In Mellor and Oliver, pp. 112–24. Originally printed in *Review of Metaphysics* 7 (1953): 3–18.

Williams, J. R. G. 2007a. Eligibility and Inscrutability. *Philosophical Review* 116.3: 361–99.

Williams, J. R. G. 2007b. The Possibility of Onion Worlds. *Australasian Journal of Philosophy* 85: 193–203.

Williamson, T. 2007. *The Philosophy of Philosophy*. Oxford: Blackwell.

Wilson, J. 2006. Review of Gonzalo Rodriguez-Pereyra's Resemblance Nominalism: A Solution to the Problem of Universals. *Philosophy and Phenomenological Research* 72.1: 241–6.

Wittgenstein, L. 1953. *Philosophical Investigations*. Oxford: Blackwell.

Wright, C. J. G. 1983. *Frege's Conception of Numbers as Objects*. Aberdeen: Aberdeen University Press.

Wright, C. J. G. 1992. *Truth and Objectivity*, Cambridge, MA: Harvard University Press.

Wright, C. J. G. 2013. A Plurality of Pluralisms. In N. Pedersen and C. D. Wright (eds.), *Truth and Pluralism: Current Debates*. New York: Oxford University Press, pp. 123–56.

Yablo, S. 1992. Mental Causation. *The Philosophical Review* 101.2: 245–80.

Yablo, S. 1996. How In the World? *Philosophical Topics* 24.1: 255–86.

Index